4301 THIRD STREET
TILLAMOOK, OREGON 97141
PH 503.842.8222

WRITING FROM SCRATCH

WRITING FROM SCRATCH
Freelancing

JOHN CALDERAZZO

JOHN CLARK PRATT
General Editor, *Writing from Scratch* Series

ROWMAN & LITTLEFIELD PUBLISHERS, INC.

ROWMAN & LITTLEFIELD PUBLISHERS, INC.

Published in the United States of America
by Rowman & Littlefield Publishers, Inc.
8705 Bollman Place, Savage, Maryland 20763

British Cataloging in Publication Information Available

Library of Congress Cataloging-in-Publication Data

Calderazzo, John.
Writing from scratch : freelancing / John Calderazzo.
p.   cm. — (Writing from scratch series)
Includes bibliographical references.
1. Authorship.   2. Freelance journalism.   I. Title.   II. Series.
PN153.C35   1990
808'.02—dc20   90-9084 CIP
ISBN 0–8476–7633–1   cloth

5   4   3   2   1

Printed in the United States of America

For SueEllen
and my writing students

Contents

Preface ix

A Definition xi

A Fable xiii

1. Getting Started 1

   Finding the Penguin Room (and Other Sources
   of Inspiration)

2. Getting Information 7

   Noodling, Dumb Luck, and the Eloquence of Facts

3. Getting More Information 23

   Being There: How to Interview

4. Getting It Done 41

   Writing and Re-writing and Re-writing and . . .

5. Actors in the Sky 63

6. Getting It Out . . . Getting It Back 79

   How to Prepare a Manuscript and What to Do When It
   Comes Back

7. Getting It Done *Again* 85

   Resubmit • Resell • Rejoice

Good Books 99

Endnotes 103

Preface

JOHN CALDERAZZO WRITES of the "eloquence of facts," but he also demonstrates his own remarkable eloquence in this book that shows what freelancing is all about. All the necessary how-to's are here—but even more important is the profile that emerges of an aware, perceptive writer whose words turn everyday occurrences into fascinating, salable articles.

There's something here for everyone: the beginning, would-be writer, the experienced but not-yet-famous scribe, even the blocked or jaded professional who needs a new inspiration, a new direction. For the mid-career journalist, for instance, chapter seven, "Getting It Done *Again*," adds a dimension that many, if not most, people who've been selling their work might never have considered.

Throughout this book, Calderazzo's wry, unselfconscious humor makes *Writing from Scratch: Freelancing* an absolute joy to read. This man *loves* writing—but more important, he loves the people and places he writes about. Consequently, one learns not only just what a freelancer does, but also what all successful serious writers must never lose: the humanity and compassion that make creativity possible.

This book is remarkable. There's not another one like it.

John Clark Pratt
General Editor

A Definition

free·lance

n. 1. A PERSON, ESP. A WRITER or an artist, who sells services to employers without a long-term commitment to any one of them. 2. ONE WHO REMAINS UNCOMMITTED to a party, such as a magazine or newspaper or advertising agency, and proceeds independently, sometimes perilously, while friends and family look on in horror or, occasionally, admiration. 3. A MEDIEVAL MERCENARY, a part- or full-time professional soldier in the war of words who, fueled by curiosity, runs off tilting at windmills, pen or word processor poised. 4. AN IMPOSSIBLE ROMANTIC (like that most famous windmill-tilter of all, Don Quixote) who is also . . . 5. A SURVIVOR, a practical thinker (like Quixote's sidekick, Sancho Panza). 6. AN INSPIRED RESEARCHER, willing to leave no page unturned and no interview unfinished in pursuit of a story, such as the one you will read in this book. 7. A HARDY TRAVELER in the physical world and in the imagination (although, when writing nonfiction, never making it up). 8. A DAMN HARD WORKER, willing to write and rewrite ferociously, to get it right. 9. A STORYTELLER, since one of the greatest appeals of all compelling prose, fiction or nonfiction, is a good story. The story in this book, for instance, of how I wrote a single nonfiction article, from the moment I was inspired by an exciting idea, through my background research, my interviews with some very unusual people, my notetaking, organizing, writing, rewriting, manuscript preparation and submission, and, finally, the publishing that all writers work for. 10. ME, as will become obvious in this book, which I hope you enjoy. 11. YOU?

A Fable

ONCE THERE WAS a little boy who had no idea what he wanted to be when he grew up.

True, he often said that riding on a fire truck might be nice, but this was mainly to keep grown-ups happy. It was too hard to explain that sometimes he felt like, oh, just collecting the shoes that seemed to magically appear, dusty and alone, alongside the road. (It probably beat sitting in an office.) At other times, though, he thought he might grow up to be a professional boomerang thrower. Or maybe a world-class gravedigger. Or a stunt double who fell off runaway stage-coaches. Or a foreign correspondent, a doctor, an emergency room nurse, a rainforest scientist, a rock star, a spaghetti inventor, or a few other things that sounded pretty exciting.

Years later, when he had learned that the world was even more full of possibilities than he had thought as a child, he *still* had no idea what he wanted to be.

So he became a freelance writer.

Chapter 1

Getting Started

Finding the Penguin Room
(and Other Sources of Inspiration)

WHAT'S THE BEST way to get started writing?

The answer is simple. *Find the Penguin Room.*

The explanation, though, is a bit complicated: During my career as a freelance writer, I've published essays and articles about all kinds of topics—about a man who took his own life in jail, a man who compiled a record collection that would stack up higher than the Empire State Building, the woman who helped start China's save-the-panda program, the man who makes the Swiss Army knife, a "creative leisuring" specialist, a squirrel that acted like a mouse—about fighting spring floods, running, hiking, cross-country skiing, caving, and dozens of other subjects. Yet no matter what I write about, long before I jot down a word or punch my first shaky sentence into a computer, I always seem to find myself in the place that I now call the Penguin Room.

Writer's Inspiration

This is the place that inspires and strengthens me for the exciting but often tough job of seeing my self-doubts, my research, my writing—and *re*-writing—through to the end. As far as I can tell, it's also the place that inspires most writers who care at all about what they're doing, whether they're newspaper reporters or novelists, prize-winning veterans or beginners. In fact, whether or not you know it, you've probably already spent some time in the Penguin Room yourself.

But how do you know when you're there? And what am I talking about, anyway?

Let me explain by describing a surprising trip I took not long ago— a writing assignment that led me to a story that was quite different from the one I went to write, and to a room that really *was* reserved for penguins.

Last spring, I flew from my home in Colorado to Salt Lake City, Utah, then drove a rental car to the small desert town of Moab, which sits far off by itself in the southeast corner of the state. I was on a freelance writing assignment for *Chevrolet Friends,* a national travel magazine that I'd frequently written for. My job was to explore the red-rock canyons and beautiful stone arches that have made the Moab area famous, then write about the trip. It was not exactly the worst assignment of my career. Every day for about a week, I took long hikes through steep-walled gulches, along sun-burnt cliffs, and over and around boulders the size of houses. The brisk, clear weather was invigorating, and as I took in the spectacular scenery I had to keep reminding myself that someone was actually *paying* me for all this. Then came the surprise.

One evening, as I was waiting for some pizza in a downtown Moab restaurant, I glanced around for something to read. This was partly a life-long habit (I'll generally read anything I can get my eyes on, and especially when I'm waiting to eat). But it was also professional instinct. Looking at a bulletin board or leafing through even the flimsiest local newspaper is one of the fastest ways I know to learn about a new town. (Much more on this kind of research later.) Soon a bright yellow flyer on a nearby table caught my eye.

Grand Opening!

HOLLYWOOD STUNTMEN'S HALL OF FAME

June 23–25 Moab, Utah

Even though I was tired and a bit dehydrated from the day's hike, I felt a bolt of energy shoot through me. Stuntmen?

As a kid, I'd been fascinated by the men and women who tumbled out of cars and jumped from cliffs in the movies and on TV. How could they do those things without breaking their necks? What did these brave and probably crazy people look like, anyway? And now it turned out that in only a couple of months they'd be opening their own Hall of Fame—just like baseball players.

Did a stunt artist have to fall off at least 500 horses to get voted in? What would the Hall display—crutches and casts? And, my biggest question of all: Why was it opening in Moab, a uranium boom town gone bust, a place so far from big cities that from a nearby hill you could see the last mountain range surveyed in the lower forty-eight states?

Following Your Curiosity

By nine the next morning I was at the address listed on the back of the flyer. It was an old brick church that looked newly renovated. Since there was no doorbell, I knocked a couple of times, got no response, then nudged open some double glass doors and walked into a large, high-ceilinged foyer. (Curiosity may have killed the cat, but it sure can help a writer. More on this—plus compensating for shyness—later, too.)

Right away I noticed some square concrete slabs leaning against a wall. One of them bore the imprint of cowboy boots, and, in script: "Roy Rogers." Under that, .45 caliber bullets formed the letters "RR." Other slabs had names like John Wayne, Burt Reynolds, Kim "Wonder Woman" Renee, Chuck "The Rifleman" Connors. There was even one for the guy who played Darth Vader in the "Star Wars" fight scenes. I glanced up. From an interior room, a dummy in a spider mask and black cape was crashing in stop-time through a shattering window.

Thinking Like a Freelancer

Somewhere in my freelance writer's head, a little flywheel started to turn. Although it had been years since I'd sat through a western or a swashbuckler (I'd switched to European films in which nobody ever gets clonked on the head), this place was starting to look interesting. I was already thinking of giving it a paragraph or two in a "local attractions" sidebar, or connected story, to the Moab hiking piece. But maybe there was enough here—or in the upcoming "Grand Opening"—to merit its own story.

Soon I wandered into a basement office where I found a young woman hunched intently over a computer screen. After about a minute of cheerful conversation, I established that her name was Robbie Swasey and that she knew practically everything there was to know about this place, making her a terrific source. She knew everything because she was the do-it-all assistant to the Hall's founder, a movie and TV stuntman named John Hagner. And, best of all, she just happened to be in the middle of confirming the Grand Opening guest list, which included old friends of John's like Iron Eyes Cody (who must have been in every cowboy and Indian movie of my childhood, maybe even my *father's* childhood) and Bert Goodrich, the first Mr. America, from way back in 1939. I also learned that dozens of westerns, from John Ford classics to Grade Z shoot-em-ups, had been filmed in the area. The little flywheel in my head whirred faster.

You may be wondering how I got all this information so quickly. Easy. I did what anyone could do, experienced writer or not: I simply asked Robbie about things that genuinely interested me. (You'd be *amazed* at what you'll find out just by showing a little curiosity and thus flattering people with your attention. In fact, if you're not curious, you might as well forget about being a writer right now.)

After a few more minutes, and before I'd had a chance to tell Robbie I was a freelance writer (which I don't always mention immediately, since it can make some people stiffen up), she stood and said, "I need a break. Want to see the place?"

With these golden words, we were off. The tour took a while. I'll spare you the details except to say that we strolled through a series of almost-completed museum rooms devoted to the history of stunts. The Hall was interesting, all right, but, I decided with some disappointment, not *quite* interesting enough to make the flywheel in my head whisper the words I had hoped to hear, that message familiar to all veteran writers (especially busy ones, who must carefully choose potential projects): "You MUST write this story, You MUST write this story, You MUST . . ."

On the way back to Robbie's office, I was already thinking of her generous mini-tour as a nice way to spend a morning, but maybe not much more, when we strolled past an open doorway. Then she said, almost as an afterthought, "And this is the Penguin Room . . ."

"*Penguin* Room?"

"Right," she said casually, as though it were a broom closet. "John happened to be on one of Admiral Byrd's expeditions to the South Pole, and he's been collecting penguins ever since. I guess he's got hundreds of them in storage, so pretty soon now they'll have their own display room."

I backtracked a few steps and poked my head through the doorway. It was simply a square room, newly painted and perfectly empty. Even though I knew Robbie was talking about stuffed penguins, for a gleeful moment I had a vision of these absurd South Pole birds waddling in their dinner jackets across the top of a Utah mesa, a coyote or two howling in the distance. I could just see them—hundreds strong!—wobbling happily in single file through sagebrush and cactus as John Wayne and maybe a thousand Apaches looked on.

What kind of person, I wondered, brings a penguin collection to the broiling slickrock desert? Who was this guy who just "happened" to be on an expedition to one of the last great unexplored places on earth?

The flywheel in my head was suddenly whirring like mad. And even though I had planned to devote the middle of my summer to writing stories that were more "serious" or "literary" than this one promised to be, by the time I said goodbye to Robbie, I knew that I'd be back in June for the Grand Opening.

This, then—this excitement about the amusing and the unusual—was the inspiration for the story that you're going to see me research and write during the next few chapters. You'll see a wide range of my techniques: from interviews with Hollywood stunt men and women, to library and other kinds of research (like my attempt at a stunt artist "test"), to my clumsy, early writing drafts, to the very different and far more accomplished (I hope) final manuscript for submission to a national magazine. Along the way, I'll try to talk about much of what I've learned as a widely published, self-supporting freelance writer—knowledge that may help you write and publish your first story or perhaps push you beyond occasional publication to a full-time career. More than anything, I'll try to talk about what makes good writing and what it really feels like to be a freelance writer, with all its joys and frustrations.

For reasons that you'll soon see, the stunt artist story also turned out to be a tougher, more personal and more "serious" project than I'd figured on.

The Story That You Must Tell

Not that I really had much choice in the matter. My little stroll with Robbie had led me to the Penguin Room—not just a room in Moab, Utah, but that much larger, more pliable space in the imagination where so many writers spend so much of their lives, where *you* do, too, or will soon enough. It's the place you live in when you realize that you've come upon a story, however meaningless or strange it may seem to others, that keeps you awake at night and dreaming much of the day, a story that you, more than anyone else, MUST tell.

"Write as if you were dying," says essayist Annie Dillard. "At the same time, assume you write for an audience consisting solely of terminal patients. That is, after all, the case. What would you begin writing if you knew you would die soon? What could you say to a dying person that would not enrage by its triviality?"[1] So . . .

Welcome to the Penguin Room. It's a strangely pleasant kind of prison. And you escape from it not with a metal file, but with pen and paper, not by digging a tunnel, but by writing, writing, writing your way out.

Chapter 2

Getting Information

Noodling, Dumb Luck, and the Eloquence of Facts

I'VE NEVER CARED for "research."

I mean the word itself, which makes me think of an airless basement stuffed with thick, unreadable books. It also reminds me of hypodermic needles, the kind used by unsmiling technicians wearing beepers and white coats somewhere up on the sixty-third floor.

Worse, by power of association, "research" can make nonfiction writers sound like the drudges of the literary world, the metaphor-poor cousins of novelists and poets—those pure souls whose ethereal connection with the Muse precludes anything as ordinary as "digging" for facts. As though Herman Melville could have written *Moby Dick* without compiling a personal Encyclopaedia Britannica of whaling lore. As though Emily Dickinson could have "heard a fly buzz" when she "died" without having the keen eye of an entomologist.

So much for the word itself. But the *act* of researching I simply love. When I start getting really interested in a subject—say, the aerodynamics of a boomerang, or the foundations of Buddhism—I'll happily spend half the day rooting through bookstacks for the kind of information that might have gone up in flames with the ancient Library of Alexandria. Sometimes, in fact, I prefer the excitement and challenge of researching to writing itself.

The "Power" of Truth

In any case, whether I'm conducting a face-to-face interview, an odyssey through dusty file cabinets, or a survey of my own childhood memories, I'm doing something absolutely necessary to my work. Research creates the "non" in "nonfiction," and carries with it tremendous responsibilities and power.

Keep that power in mind. Ask a few friends what they like best about a magazine article that engages them, and they'll frequently say, "It's *true.*" So whenever you're frustrated about the hard work of careful research, remind yourself that what essayist E. B. White called "the eloquence of facts"[2] can often become your great advantage over writers of largely imaginative works (which are "true" in a different sense)—the novelists, short story writers and poets of the world.

This doesn't mean you're about to hear "My Ten Commandments for Fact-Finding." Researching a story isn't like tackling a problem in basic geometry. There are all kinds of complex human personalities involved, including yours. The kind of research you do depends heavily on your own interests and skills, and the circumstances of the story and its main characters.

Not to mention dumb luck.

A few years ago, when I was living in Ohio, I drove from my home near Bowling Green to the little river town of Grand Rapids to research a feature story for *Ohio Magazine* about a disastrous flood that had poured through Main Street several months earlier. I was tired from the drive, so I made my first stop the candy counter at the drug store. The druggist turned out to be a man who'd taken it upon himself to measure the height of the river—every day for years. During the days leading up to the flood he'd measured it by the hour. By the time I'd finished my candy bar, he had provided me with a dramatic eyewitness account of the rising waters. He eventually became a major character in the story I wrote (I called him The Man Who Measures the River).

He also seemed to know everyone in town, and the list of names and phone numbers he gave me saved hours of the often frustrating legwork that initiates this kind of research. And all because of a sweet tooth. Any veteran writer has a dozen similar stories.

So instead of laying down some laws of research that may or may not work for you, let me show you what happened as I gathered information for my story on Hollywood stunt artists.

Where Research Really Starts

My research for this story-to-be began the moment I realized I wanted to write it.

Robbie and I still had our heads in the Penguin Room when I told her that I was interested in coming back to write about the Grand Opening. Or the Hall. Or her boss John Hagner. Or . . . well, whatever turned out to be interesting. One reason I told her about my intentions, vague as they were, was just to be honest. After all, the story seemed uncomplicated and "friendly," hardly requiring the undercover tactics of Watergate reporters Woodward and Bernstein.

Background Information

Robbie looked delighted, and within minutes I was back in her office paging through a sheaf of news releases about the Grand Opening, fact sheets about the history of the Hall, and copies of a stunt artist newsletter written by John. This wealth of data that I could take home to absorb at my leisure was of course the *other* reason I mentioned I was a writer.

As I hastily stuffed the papers into my daypack (which reminded me why I'd come to Moab in the first place), I knew that not a single sentence of this background information might make it into my finished story. Nevertheless, I also knew that this was one of the first steps in sound research. Although fact sheets and news releases usually reflect "the company line," they can also help you begin to understand your subject.

Interviewing

More important, they prepare you for interviews. For instance, now that I could read up on the history of the Hall of Fame, I could avoid sounding like an amateur later on and wasting John Hagner's time and mine by asking obvious questions. Or, I could try an old interviewing trick and *purposely* ask him the obvious just to make sure he had his facts straight or to see what kind of extra or "slant" information he could add to the basics.

Now and then, this trick also lets me pretend to jot down an
interviewee's words, while what I'm really writing are observations
like: "Has craggy face & crooked broken-looking nose. Stunt accident? Blue eyes light up when he talks about old movies—probably
loves nostalgia." Here are some of the things I scribbled down while I
was talking with Robbie in her office:

> In R's office, walls are hung
> w/ framed letters of celebs:
>
> The Lone Ranger – Clayton Moore
> (xerox of him rearing up on Silver)
>
> Montie Montana (??) – his name
> is printed in rope script at top
> of letters . . .

Using the Phone

Before I left Robbie, I got John's home phone number, in case it
was unlisted, and asked if the office had an 800 number. Small outfits
rarely do, yet I always ask since it can save lots of money later in long
distance bills. (Your phone company can tell you how to buy a national
toll-free directory which will pay for itself quickly. Most libraries have
them, too. There is also an 800 information number: 1-800-555-
1212.)

I did *not* tell Robbie that I would put the Hall of Fame on the cover
of *Life,* or that I had angle X, Y or Z in mind for the story. I don't
have that kind of pull, unfortunately. And it was much too early to
establish any angles at all for the story.

What NOT to Tell Your Interview Subject

Besides, you should almost never tell your subjects, no matter how sympathetic or "friendly," precisely what you're going to write. It can set up false expectations or limit your responses. Worse, it can put you in the position of "pleasing" your subject—which isn't your job as a writer at all. Your job is to be truthful and, if possible, please *yourself*. You are, after all, your own ultimate reader.

If you cave in to any of these threats to honest reporting, your story might sound like a PR release. And if that's all you're after, you may as well work for a big advertising agency and at least make a steady salary. So whenever I'm asked what I'm intending to write, I try to be as general as possible: "Oh, a profile of the place, I guess." Actually, I could hardly be more specific. As you'll soon see, stories tend to change as they unfold on the page.

Next, I tried to talk to John Hagner, to feel him out. If I found him unbearably boring, I might drop the idea of coming back to the desert in the broiling heat of June.

Deciding if a Source Is Worth Interviewing

I also wanted to make sure he was willing to talk openly. Sometimes sources will reveal only canned or obvious information because they're nervous about something—say, a pending secret investigation.

Or they feel they've been burned by the press. This was the case with a former high-profile sheriff I once interviewed about a prisoner who committed suicide in the sheriff's jail. The sheriff felt that he lost his re-election bid, then his marriage, partly because of unfair newspaper stories about his role in the tragedy. By the time I caught up with him, 1200 miles away over the telephone, he'd erected a Great Wall of China around himself. Face to face, I might have been able to break through, but the impersonality of the phone created additional barriers, and I didn't get much.

Or sometimes a source, usually a public figure, wants to protect information he or she has promised to a biographer or a ghost writer for an "autobiography." You know the kind:

Scrooge McDuck: The Secret Life of a Zillionaire
(As Told to Geraldo Rivera)

Finally, I thought I'd try to catch John before I left town to save myself a few phone bills later, especially because I had no idea yet what magazine, if any, I'd try to convince to support me on this project. (Since most freelancers are in many ways working for themselves, it helps to be as naturally cheap as I am.)

No luck in finding John, though. But I did get his home answering machine. On came some music, the kind of swelling, rousing score that I suddenly remembered from the big fight scenes in old westerns, the kind of music I hadn't heard in years. Then: "Hi. This is John Hagner. I'm out on the back lot. Or I'm out on location. Or I'm just plain *out* . . ."

I found myself smiling. Most "creative" phone messages simply annoy me. But Hagner sounded witty. Also, the music sent me back to the almost criminally carefree Saturday afternoons of my childhood—a nice break from my usual adult worries about cancer, nuclear bombs, and world environmental disaster.

Sure, I told myself as I drove out of Moab, June sounds like a fine time of year to come back to the desert.

*   *   *

Back home in Colorado, I immediately return to doing what most freelance writers I know do—being ringmaster to the flying circus of the writing life, juggling a chaos of letters, phone calls, writing projects, ideas for future stories, and part-time editing or teaching jobs.

Actually, this isn't quite true. Recently, my life has been less chaotic than when I was exclusively a freelancer. During the last few years I've taught fiction and nonfiction classes at Colorado State University in Fort Collins—a full-time job. Being a professor limits my writing time. Yet, like more and more writers who have "gone into" the university, I find that it helps me choose the stories I really want to pursue since I no longer have to pay the rent, or my own health insurance, strictly by writing.

So now I work on a schedule that probably sounds familiar to most people who write. I slap down the sentences mostly during vacations and weekends and squeeze in some scribbling around the edges of my normal work day. This schedule also of course gives me an excuse to complain about not having enough time to write.

But back to the research. A day or two after I return home, I get through to John Hagner. We chat for a couple of minutes about the Grand Opening, and he tells me about some newly confirmed guests, including Lee Aakers, who played the little boy on what was once one of my favorite TV shows, "Rin Tin Tin." (I've always wondered what happens to child stars.)

"Breaking Through" an Interview

John is friendly and enthusiastic, but I hardly write down a note. His speech seems tinged with the fulsome, slightly elevated language of a veteran press agent. This has me a little worried, since professional smoothness often yields only superficial quotations and not a whole lot about the flesh and blood person doing the talking. I can't really blame him. I'm The Press and he obviously wants all the publicity he can get. Meeting him in person later on might help me break through, but you can never tell. Then I glance down at the list of questions I've written out before the phone call—an old habit. I ask John how he first got interested in stunt artists.

He pauses—the first time there's been any break in his patter—and then begins to tell me about his childhood in Baltimore, and how those flickering Saturday afternoons in the local moviehouse sparked his imagination. Almost immediately, I notice a change in the way he speaks. His voice deepens, becomes more intimate—even though each sentence seems to carry him further away from me, back into his own long-gone childhood. Soon he's speaking straight from the heart, about things he obviously cares about deeply.

"I see," I say, now scribbling like mad. "Yeah. Sure, I understand. Yes, yes, yes . . ."

SUSAN GOODMAN
FREELANCING (AND LISTENING) FROM HOME

You might call it The Fifteen Percent Solution. "If you get to write about things you really like at least fifteen percent of the time, you're probably doing OK," says Susan Goodman. "Then there's the rest of the work."

A professional approach to the "rest of the work," she implies, makes the difference between the romantic myth of writing and the reality of the market, between a freelance career and dabbling, between "doing OK" and sinking. Goodman seems to be doing more than OK. She writes full-time out of her Boston home and purposely "skates around" from topic to topic—travel, humor, food, science, medicine, and offbeat subjects such as The World Future Society. She's a contributor to travel magazines and national markets like *Harper's Bazaar, Parents,* and *Glamour.*

She likes working at home because "it's here," it allows her to spend more time with her young child, and it reduces expenses. It's also flexible. "I can work fifteen minutes here, twenty there, and I can run upstairs at 10 p.m. and call California," she says.

On the other hand, California can call back at any time. "The disadvantage is that you're never far from work. There are enough distractions that unless you have discipline you can easily fall behind. I also sometimes miss associating with others, a source of inspiration and creativity."

Goodman is a former social worker who hated her job and "just started writing." She published her first story, a feature about the ways in which various ethnic groups celebrate Thanksgiving, in the *Boston Herald,* and she used that clip and others to go on from there. She thinks part of her success comes from wanting to really listen to people. "Nobody ever listens to anyone anymore unless they're famous," she says. "I try to make someone I'm interviewing think they are special. The beauty of freelancing is that you can just sit down with people and let them blossom and flower."[3]

Getting Background Information

During our phone interview, John mentions several old movies that were well before my time, so as soon as I hang up I reach for one of the reference books I always keep near my desk at home (see Good Books at the end of the book for a helpful list).

The easy-to-use *Writer's Resource Guide* from Writer's Digest Books is a directory of sources of information on practically any subject. It's a great starting point for the freelance writer who needs a little bit of information quickly. In a couple of minutes I find three or four potentially good sources for background information, like the Old Time Western Film Club of Siler, North Carolina.

And this typical entry:

252• LOUIS B. MAYER LIBRARY, THE AMERICAN FILM INSTITUTE
Box 27999, 2021 N. Western Ave., Los Angeles CA 90027. (213)856-7655, 856-7656. Contact: **Reference Desk. Description:** Reading, reference and research library "primarily devoted to motion pictures, televison and video. Seeks to provide documentation and information covering

such topics as history, aesthetics, biography, production and business aspects.'' **Services:** Provides advisory, bibliographical, historical, how-to, technical and trade information. Offers library facilities and telephone reference services. Library collection includes 5,500 books on all aspects of motion pictures, TV and video as well as selected titles on photography, theatre, costume design, stage plays and short stories. Other reference materials include clipping files on the entertainment industry; film festival files; screenplays and TV scripts; oral history transcripts. Publications include *Checklist of Books on Scriptwriting* (free); *Script Checklist* ($23). **How to Contact:** Write or visit. Call ''if necessary.'' Responds to inquiries as soon as possible. ''All materials must be used in the library proper.'' **Tips:** Recent information requests: ''Who wrote *Raiders of the Lost Ark*?''; ''What does a treatment look like?''; ''Where can I find an agent?''

Library Research

A few days later, when I find some free time at school, I dash off to the CSU library. Now, since the Grand Opening is almost three months away, you may be wondering why I need to do background work so soon—or anytime, since I'm planning to go back. All I can say is that I tend to work best when I follow my curiosity. And my curiosity, in its insistent way, says: "Start reading." If this is a character flaw, I indulge it happily.

Noodling

Besides, I want to start "noodling." Noodling, says author and former *Saturday Review* editor Norman Cousins, is something writers have got to do an awful lot of before putting words down on paper, since no one can write in a vacuum. He explains the process well: "You let your subconscious fill up like a reservoir, and then you discover there's an almost automatic process of sorting and developing that goes on inside you. It gets to the point where it's like trying to hold back the tide."[4]

While that tide inside me builds, I also want to see if any of the magazines I might conceivably write for have recently "done" some aspect of the topic, making it a waste of time for me to send something to them.

Overcoming Shyness

You should keep in mind that among the many hidden bonuses of doing background research—such as the satisfaction of simply learning a lot—is one antidote to shyness. If you hate calling up perfect strangers (as I used to) or simply don't know how to walk up to someone with your Twenty Most Penetrating Questions, you can compensate in part with keen bookwork. So while you're honing your interviewing skills (see next chapter), remember that strong scholarship and acute thinking can make up for a lot.

The Card Catalogue

My first stop in the library is the card catalogue, which is in the process of being computerized. (This will eventually speed me up but deprive me of the fun of picking through the cards and shoving the wooden drawers in and out.) In the subject file I look up, in this order:

> stunt artists
> stuntmen
> stunts
> Hagner, John
> Cody, Iron Eyes
> Goodrich, Bert
> Canutt, Yakima

Yakima Canutt—whose name I love—is someone I discovered in John Hagner's newsletter. He was a 1920s rodeo star who became one of the greatest stuntmen of all time. He created dozens of dangerous tricks, such as falling between a team of runaway horses, which he perfected in classic movies like John Ford's "Stagecoach." He died a couple of years ago, of simple old age, but until I browsed through the newsletter, I'd never heard of him. Now I want to know more.

A few minutes of card riffling turn up nothing. That doesn't concern me, though, because a few dead ends, parts of any research process, tend to crank up my curiosity. So, I widen my scope:

> movies
> Hollywood
> television

Unfortunately, even these fat categories don't reveal much that I want. Nor do the author and title files, where I search for *Falling for Stars,* John Hagner's aptly titled book about stunt artists, which I also learned about in the Hall of Fame newsletter.

NEWSLETTERS

A few years ago I read a newsletter for competitive boomerang throwers entitled "The Leading Edge." I became so fascinated by their wacky articulateness—they called one trophy the Douglas MacArthur "I Shall Return" Cup—that I eventually wrote and sold four articles on the subject. (See chapter seven for slanting articles to different markets.)

Whether they're hand-drawn mimeos or computer-designed printouts, distributed to a few dozen diehards or bulk mailed to thousands, newsletters are microscopes that let you see new wrinkles in things you thought you knew all about, or whole worlds you probably never knew existed. *The Blind Bowler,* circulation 2600, is the house organ of the American Blind Bowlers Association. *Bigfoot News* comes from the Sasquatch Investigators of Mid-America. *Halo Everybody!,* published by the Angel Collectors Club of America, "Promotes the collection of angels in any form." And one of my favorite titles ever comes from the newsletter of the Iron Overload Diseases Association of West Palm Beach, Florida: *Ironic Blood.*

You can find most of these—and thousands more—in the fascinating *Oxbridge Directory of Newsletters* in the reference section of your library.

But now, coming up empty-handed after all of fifteen minutes' work, I begin to experience something else I'm familiar with—annoyance at my own university's two-million-volume collection reduced so quickly to the size of a dollhouse bookshelf: The Incredible Shrinking Library.

Of course, I know that this is the nature of libraries. Most of them, like most people, have all sorts of gaps in their knowledge. (The main culprits are usually money and space.)

So I let myself whine for a few seconds about not living closer to the Library of Congress and its infinity of books. Then I get back to work, reminding myself that libraries also have hidden *strengths*— often many more than most of us realize.

For example, if I choose instead to look up drainage systems in Zimbabwe or novels about the Vietnam war, I know I'll find books by the boxful. CSU, originally an agricultural school, happens to be a center for international agronomy. And because of the interests and energy of just a few of its faculty, it also houses the largest collection of imaginative Vietnam War literature anywhere—about 1200 titles, plus 2000 miscellaneous pieces, including unpublished manuscripts. (I got these last facts expressly for this book. It took about two minutes, and I never left my desk at home. I simply called up the special collections librarian and asked. This is what I meant earlier when I said that how you research depends partly on your personality—for all but the toughest or most sensitive interviews, I've learned to be quite comfortable on the phone, and fast.)

What I'm trying to say is that, in the early stages of research, you can never tell what's "in the neighborhood." If you happen to live in, say, Toledo, Ohio, you can walk into the downtown public library and the Toledo Museum of Art and discover more about glassmaking than you can learn almost anywhere else in the world, except, perhaps, in the little town of Corning, New York, which has *another* wonderful glass museum. If it's Birmingham, Alabama, you can stroll over to the American Truck Historical Society and learn about Mack trucks and much, much more.

The Reference Desk

My next stop is the reference desk. Mostly out of curiosity, I leaf through the *Directory of Special Libraries and Information Centers,* one of at least a dozen similar guides in the library. I write down the addresses and phone numbers of a few places I didn't notice in *Writer's Resource Guide*—in a world of more than five billion people who are multiplying much too fast, no single reference covers *everything.* Next, I check a guide to Colorado libraries to see if there are any relevant special collections within driving distance. Nope.

On to *Books in Print,* which you can find in every library and most bookstores worthy of the name. By subject, title, and author this indispensible reference lists forthcoming and in-print (i.e., orderable) books from no less than 25,900 publishers.

Under "Stunt Flying" I find ten titles. But since I don't feel like burying myself yet in this one small aspect of the stunt world, I write down only a couple of names. Under "Stunt Men" I find three books. One's for "Gr 4 & up," part of a "Dangerous Jobs" series that doesn't seem worth a look now but might later if I get around to writing the children's books I've been fantasizing about for years. Into my notebook it goes. Another, *Stuntmen and Special Effects,* is part of the "Ripley's Believe It or Not" series. In it goes—you can always count on "Ripley's" to fill up your "weird facts" file.

By now, things are looking up. Even though CSU doesn't own any of these books, I know that during the next few weeks I can get at least some of them through the interlibrary loan networks that CSU belongs to. (A good reason, by the way, to start any kind of research *early.*)

Local Libraries

But what if you live in Tinytown, U.S.A., or don't have access to a fancy university library?

Don't despair; it often matters less than you think. Often, even the dinkiest branches of your town or county library offer similar arrangements with the biggest collections in the state. And most public (and some private) colleges and universities issue free or inexpensive library cards to non-students—a little-known return on your tax dollars.

Asking for Help

While I'm filling out some interlibrary loan requests, I decide to ask the reference librarian about movie and TV encyclopedias. This, I realize about thirty seconds into the conversation, is a mistake. I should have hit her up for help *the minute I walked in the door.*

In my know-it-all zeal, I somehow forgot one of my bylaws for sound research:

Go Straight to the Experts.

And like most reference librarians, this woman is an expert, an Information Prospector adept at prying facts from the deepest, darkest veins of the building. If I'd only asked, she could have saved me several dead ends and lots of time.

Local Experts

And don't forget about all the experts who live or work in your community *outside of* libraries. For instance, in the case of my community, the university, I have at my fingertips the knowledge of hundreds of professors and professional researchers, not to mention their personal libraries—a whole campus of special collections! At most colleges and universities, the office of publications or its equivalent keeps an updated file for the press on resident experts on almost every subject imaginable.

Data Bases

So now I ask the research librarian about something I've been a little embarrassed by for several weeks—some new, fancy-looking computer terminals that I can't make work despite what looks like idiot-proof instructions. Like most baby-boomers, I do most of my writing on a word processor, but I'm at heart an old, pound-the-typewriter-with-two-fingers guy, forever trying to get comfortable with new technology. (You are no doubt ahead of me here.)

Anyway, these terminals are attached to an information system called INFOTRAC. And as soon as the librarian shows me how to work one of the things (she never even rolls her eyes), I know that I have fallen in love.

With INFOTRAC.

This catalogue of contemporary newspapers, magazines and journals—hundreds of them, from *A +* *(The Independent Guide for Apple Computing)* to *Yale Review*—is roughly the electronic equivalent to *Reader's Guide to Periodical Literature,* that indispensible friend of free-lance writers like me, who often need a quick overview of many different topics.

PlinkPlinkPlink. Into the subject file under "STUNT MEN AND WOMEN" I go, and out come all kinds of things, including:

> Biography (9 entries, including bios of some folks I've never heard of AND *Newsweek* obit of Yakima Canutt!!)
> Cases (injury lawsuits—I hadn't thought of this—does this mean they can't get insurance?)
> Conduct of Life ("Like her mom, pole sitter Mellissa Sanders falls for a groundling." Huh?)

Personal Narratives (my favorite title—"The Bruise Brothers"—
about motorcycle stuntmen)
Performances (entries from *New York Times Magazine, People,
Amusement Business*—good stuff since our library probably carries all 3 mags)
Training (school for stunts—hmmm . . . "Cliff Diving III" down
at the Vo-Tech? Hahaha.)

In all, there are a dozen entries—hours and hours' worth of reading
if I care to scour the shelves or crank through the microfilm—and a
home-made booklet next to the terminals tells me which of the
indexed periodicals CSU carries. (Periodicals can be very expensive,
so libraries vary hugely on their holdings. Never expect to find
everything you need, when you need it.) All of this takes just ten
minutes to call up on the terminal and print out. If similar, perhaps
more modest versions of this system aren't already operating in larger
public libraries, they certainly will be soon.

I walk away from those terminals feeling that I've somehow already
said goodbye to my old friend, *The Reader's Guide,* and its many dog-
eared, brick-heavy volumes.

That's progress, though.

And that's the nature of libraries—and sometimes even "facts"
themselves, which, depending on what keys you try in what locks,
seem to contract and expand with the surprising, surreal rhythms of
Alice in Wonderland.

*   *   *

By now you're probably saying: What? All this work for just one
lousy article?

Well, for several reasons, that's not really the case. First, I haven't
worked particularly hard. After all, I discovered the Hall of Fame
while I was employed—if you could call it that—on an assignment
that had me hiking through some of the most spectacular country
anywhere. Second, the library search was enlightening and took only
about three hours, including the time I spent reading and xeroxing a
few of the articles I found in INFOTRAC. Finally, who's to say that
only one small piece of writing will come out of my efforts? Maybe all
my "noodling" and my trip to the Grand Opening will eventually swell
into a book or at least several articles.

Two weeks after my illuminating afternoon in the library, *Falling for
Stars* arrives (from John Hagner's hometown Baltimore Public Li-

brary, coincidentally) via interlibrary loan. A few days later, another newsletter comes from John. In the meantime, I teach classes, grade student papers, grade papers, grade papers, think about writing the hiking piece that originally took me to Moab, wonder about the Grand Opening of the Hall of Fame, think about how as a child I used to practice falling off fences with an Indian arrow in my chest . . .

In other words, I'm starting to noodle around. And the tide keeps rising.

Chapter 3

Getting More Information

Being There: How to Interview

DURING THE LAST few years, in pursuit of stories I've wanted to write, I have:

- skied past a herd of bison in the Geyser Basin of Yellowstone National Park
- walked along elephant trails in a rainforest in Thailand
- wandered through thoroughbred horse barns in Kentucky's Bluegrass Country
- camped with two dozen Tarahumara Indians on their first trip outside the remote Mexican mountain caves they call home
- picked my way with a flashlight through a cave a quarter-mile below the surface of the earth
- canoed along meandering Florida rivers

Travel, as they say, broadens the mind. It can also flatten the wallet—especially the wallet of a freelance writer who tries to finance a lot of trips without outside help.

I don't happen to be rich. That's why, except for my excursion to Thailand (which was partly covered by a university research grant), I didn't pay for any of the travel I just mentioned.

Magazines did. And they did because they'd worked with me before

and called me up with assignments I couldn't refuse. Or they agreed
to ideas I proposed to them with a query letter (a one-page description of what you'd like to write for a magazine), even though they'd
sometimes never heard of me. The result: I not only went off on
adventures I couldn't normally afford, but I also enjoyed the psycho-
logical advantage of knowing that somewhere out in that cold, cold
world beyond the circle of my friends and family, some editor was
actually *looking forward* to reading my stuff. This is the way most
experienced or full-time freelance writers try to operate.

And so, as I now think about my research trip to Moab, Utah, I
begin to calculate expenses:

> MILEAGE—700 miles round-trip, plus doodling around in Moab
> LODGING—3–4 nights of motels or campsites (no, forget the
>   camping; it'll be too hot to sleep)
> FOOD—even with a cooler of sandwiches & munchies, I'll no
>   doubt go to restaurants (I tend to brood about writing over
>   long breakfasts)
> OTHER—the usual unknowns: entrance fees, books, film, xerox-
>   ing, sun hat to replace the one that blows off a cliff, etc.

Plus the time that I'll be taking away from other, possibly more
lucrative writing projects.

Total: several hundred dollars. Not exactly a *National Geographic*
expedition to the Pole (which reminds me that I've somehow ne-
glected to ask John Hagner about his Antarctica adventure). But not
an evening at the movies, either.

Guaranteed income: zero.

To Query or Not To Query

You can see the dilemma, a frequent one for freelance writers, and
one that salaried newspaper or magazine staff writers on expense
accounts rarely face. The trip is coming up fast, but I haven't ap-
proached any magazines, mostly because I don't know what I really
want to write—a strength, as I see it. But now I wonder if I should
send off a query letter anyway, limiting myself to an angle or two of
the broad topic of stunt artists (a profile, say, of John Hagner for
People: "For 30 years, John Hagner has taken life's punches—and

thrived"), and possibly get in exchange an official assignment with its promise of traveling expenses and a fee. Or should I do what I often did when I started writing nonfiction—wing it through the research, writing, and rewriting and just hope that somebody eventually buys the thing?

With all the courage of a movie star who steps back from the ledge of a skyscraper to let his stunt double take the jump, I resolve to compromise. Mainly, I'll go on my own, footing the bills and hoping to make them up eventually—at least, come tax time, I can write them off as business expenses. But I'll also try to squeeze a few dollars from some willing publication while trying to save most of my best "material" for later.

USA TODAY looks like a good target. On the front page of the entertainment section entitled "Life," the paper runs a daily feature called "Lifeline: A Quick Read on What People Are Talking About." Emphasis on "quick." Typical entries are one-paragraph items about new books and movies, entertainment awards, appearances of celebrities, and so forth.

I've previously written a few features for other sections of the paper (one on a professional bowler, another on Denver Broncos football fans' reactions to their team's second Super Bowl defeat), so I call the editorial office, ask for a "Life" section editor, sketch in my experience, and ask if she'd like 100 or so well-chosen words about the Grand Opening.

She does—if I can cut the 100 to 75.

Why not? Surgeons aren't the only people who know how to use sharp knives. I open my thickening "STUNT" manila folder. Using an old *USA TODAY* as a model, I quickly whittle my information into this:

FALL GUY FESTIVAL

The Hollywood Stuntmen's Hall of Fame and Museum opens this week in Moab, Utah, with celebrations Thursday through Saturday. Events: Butch Cassidy Days rodeo and parade, banquet, daily stunts and film location tours. Honorees include: Iron Eyes Cody, the Indian in the famous anti-litter campaign; Bert Goodrich, the first Mr. America (1939) and Tarzan stand-in; and Lee Aakers, who played Rusty in TV's "Rin Tin Tin."

I call the Hall of Fame and ask Robbie Swasey (my original source, remember?) to double-check spellings and times, since there's no faster way to ruin your reputation than by making elementary factual errors. Then I dictate my 69 words over the phone to a *USA TODAY* editor. If my home computer had a modem (as it surely would if I were still freelancing full-time), I could zap it cross-country in milliseconds. With a few minor changes ("Thursday through Saturday" becomes "Thursday–Saturday" and the purposely alliterative "Fall Guy Festival" becomes "The Fall Guys") the item runs a couple of days later, on the day, in fact, that I leave for Moab.

This formulaic news blip certainly isn't literature, but it earns me some gas money for the trip and lets me walk into the Hall of Fame with a bit of credibility folded under my arm (the *USA TODAY* clip says, in effect: Here is a guy who knows how to connect with the national media). More important, it boosts my confidence when I need it—when, in fact, I often need it—the moment before I put my time, money and ego on the line for uncertain rewards. This is the mildly neurotic dark side of working entirely for myself and writing pretty much the way I please (when I'm not churning out news blips). The fact that a publication read by at least five million people a day thinks that the Grand Opening is newsworthy confirms for me the story's potential popular appeal.

Contacting Editors

Before I go further, a word about querying by phone. Most editors would rather hold a vampire bat to their ear than a telephone with an inquiring writer on the other end. They don't have time to chat, even if they wanted to, and they can't tell a thing about your writing without actually seeing it. I called *USA TODAY* only because a few people there had seen my writing and I knew that for small news items they often worked by phone. Even then I was surprised an editor said yes. Ninety-nine percent of the time, don't call an editor. WRITE. (Now that you know I'm not going to write a query letter, see chapter seven for good and bad ways to go about it.)

*   *   *

At last, I throw my notebooks, tape recorder and camera into the car and take off. But as I climb west through the Colorado Rockies, I find something else to fret about. Hasn't my *USA TODAY* story just alerted the writers of the world to my little secret? What if they flock to Moab and steal *my* story?

Trusting Your Own Vision

This kind of worrying (immensely egocentric, of course) rarely fails to drive me crazy. You may have had similar thoughts about one of your own projects. However, as I remind myself when I inevitably calm down, in all but a few cases—such as an investigation, where secrecy can be crucial—such overblown concerns reveal a misunderstanding of the writing process and maybe even of reality itself.

"My" story, whatever that will be, is actually only one version of the many, many versions that might be written about something. Besides my own view of things (and second and third versions of my original), there's also the story that might be written by John Hagner or any of the other stunt artists, or by someone who grew up in Moab, or by any number of visiting writers . . .

On the other hand, no matter how many larcenous, better-connected, or faster writers are skulking around the outskirts of a story, I can still make that story absolutely mine. All I have to do is trust the instincts, skills, and quirks that brought me this far as a writer and that define me as an individual.

This fact is extremely important to remember: *Whether you've published ten books or nothing at all, NOBODY sees or thinks about the world quite as you do or describes it with your "voice."*

The vigor of individual though still-emerging voices was recently shown to me by some of my CSU students. Last semester, in my undergraduate creative nonfiction writing workshop, I asked them to write about "The Life and Times of the Lory Plaza." The plaza is the large, often busy area in front of our campus's student center. I gave no other instructions—no suggestions for point of view, length, focus, audience—and I wouldn't permit any of the customary class discussion about possible approaches to the topic. Now, an assignment as vague as this one can terribly frustrate beginning writers—they might as well try nailing fog to a wall. But it was late in the semester of an intermediate-level class in which we'd explored personal voices, and I wanted to see how resourceful these semi-veterans could be.

The class rugby player, who frequently found ways to turn assignments into features about his favorite sport, wrote about the plaza from the point of view of his rugby teammates. They apparently spend their more tranquil moments lounging on the plaza and editorializing about the passing human traffic. An older student who had earlier written movingly about death and personal loss described the mood of the plaza late at night—the only sound that of a pop can rolling in the wind as the lights of the nearby library winked off one by one. A woman who liked blending background research with narration described the history of the university through events that took place on the plaza.

As a teacher, I felt good about my students' efforts. They were learning to trust their own ways of looking at the world and talking about it. As a writer and ongoing student of literature—that centuries-long line of individual voices—I wasn't a bit surprised.

So why should I worry about someone stealing "my" story? As my students so recently demonstrated, if I care enough about the material to write it in my voice, from my point of view, the story that will emerge will be virtually theft-proof.

Being There

Utah!

Red-rock country: the high slickrock desert, its sandstone towers gnarled by wind and scooped smooth by water, sun-baked, silent, and not a penguin in sight.

Here is Surprise Number One—not so much that John Hagner's legions of penguins are still packed in their boxes somewhere, but that John has never actually *been* to Antarctica. He simply served as a young Navy seaman on the huge aircraft carrier that helped support Byrd's expedition by floating in the vicinity. So much for my visions of a man squinting into a Polar gale, urging his huskies to "Mush, mush!" their way into history. (By now, you can probably see why I became a writer.) I'm not thrilled about the jumbled communication that has raised false hopes. It's John himself who sets me straight.

But I don't sulk about it, either. Because of my background research and general noodling, the topic of stunt artists has already grabbed hold of me. Besides, too many things are going on at the festival that I don't want to miss, such as Surprise Number Two: it turns out that many of the stunt veterans who've come have never met each other and so are getting acquainted by swapping stories. Good ones.

With help from my notes, let me sketch out some of the leading characters and events of these three days and my strategies for dealing with them. To avoid repeating myself later and risk losing you as a reader, I'm going to jump around a bit and leave out much of what goes into my story, which you'll be seeing soon enough.

JOHN HAGNER. A very athletic 60, easy-going despite the chaos around him. A "fights & falls" specialist, he seems willing to talk but hard to get alone because he's running the show. I figure I can fill in any gaps later by phone.

BERT GOODRICH. Worth an essay or article by himself *(Modern Maturity?)*. At 81, the first Mr. America still looks strong enough to bend me into a pretzel, and I'm fairly sturdy. He tells long engaging tales about swinging on ropes for early Tarzan actor Buster Crabbe (who later played "Flash Gordon," one of my childhood heroes) on location in the "heart of Africa"—a woodsy grove outside of Los Angeles that's now a fancy housing development . . .

Hmmm. As I write this now, I'm thinking about a story idea that didn't occur to me in Moab, a "Whatever Happened To . . ." about famous movie backdrops and landscapes. How many Sherwood Forests, Skull Islands, Yukons, and other fantasy lands are now shopping malls? On the other hand, how many became parts of National Parks? That might be an interesting angle from which to look at "development" or "growth" in this country. I could try *American Film* magazine on this, and/or *National Parks*. Or, best of all, *Smithsonian* or *American Heritage*. (See chapter seven for tips about learning the market.)

KIM RENEE. For kicks, she jumped between rooftops in the New York City neighborhood she grew up in. A former circus high flyer who sailed over trees and houses for TV's "Wonder Woman," she has introduced each of her children, on their six-month birthday, to the trapeze in her back yard. She'd make a good starting point for a story about contemporary Hollywood stuntwomen. I could include a deaf stuntwoman I read about in the most recent Hall of Fame newsletter. Huge circulation magazines like *Redbook* might pay major bucks for it. (*That* would cover my $24-a-night motel.) Or maybe describe her "high flying" kids for *Parents* or *People* feature?

WHITEY HUGHES. Great fun, great teacher/storyteller. He has worked with everyone—John Wayne, Yakima Canutt, Burt Reynolds (one of the few stunt artists who became a big star). He'll take time to explain details of how to fall off a galloping horse with minimum risk of injury. He's also an excellent source to come back to later to double-check technical details—crucial for all but the simplest stories.

His self-effacing, impish grin makes you forget about his extraordinary reflexes and courage; at age 66 he's still doing stunts. Why don't his bones break like old china?

JODY McQUEEN. Brother of the famous Steve. Wiry, rawhide-skinned car and motorcycle ace, although like the others he seems to have tried all sorts of movie mayhem. On the first day of the festival I notice him talking to Whitey Hughes, Bert Goodrich, and a few others, so I nudge my way into this loose circle and turn on my hand tape recorder.

Listening for Stories

". . . and, see, this one time I was on location for a shoot-em-up in Portland, Oregon, and the stunt crew and I went out to a little lunch place to talk things over. We were making the usual plans, saying stuff like, 'Now as soon as I start choking the Mayor, you guys gut-shoot the Sheriff . . .' Well, those waitresses must have had good ears, 'cause by the time dessert came around the place was full of state troopers standing around our table, not smiling. We had to show our IDs to get out of there."

We all laugh with Jody. I flip off the recorder. Then Whitey starts a story. I flip it back on. Then it's Bert's turn. Round and round the stories go, as steadily as the wheels of my tape recorder.

The Technology of Fact-Finding

Does my little machine bother anyone?

It doesn't seem to. And I'd be surprised if it did, because I'm very careful about the way I record facts and observations, and I'm sure Jody and the others, with a good hundred years of Hollywood under their collective belts, are used to dealing with far bigger intrusions.

Interviews are great sources of firsthand information for writers, but they can be tricky. Generally speaking, the bigger the piece of technology you haul around, the higher the chance of intimidating or changing the person you're interviewing and perhaps yourself as well. You have a wide array of approaches to choose from.

At one extreme of the scale might be the tactics used by Truman Capote and Tom Wolfe—at least according to the following stories. In what Capote later called a "finger exercise" leading up to the deadly serious research for his "nonfiction novel" *In Cold Blood,* he interviewed Marlon Brando for forty-five minutes without once pulling out a notebook. He claimed to have memorized the whole thing. While Wolfe was researching his enormously entertaining *The Electric Kool-Aid Acid Test,* about some of the roots of the hippie movement, he spent a lot of time with Ken Kesey and his band of "Merry Pranksters." Several years after the book came out, I heard Kesey talk about Wolfe. "Tom Wolfe is good," he said, pausing to let it sink in. "The whole time he was with us, he never took a note. He just *sat* there, glomming it all in."

That may have been Kesey's honest impression, but he of course was slightly preoccupied. In a brief but telling author's note at the end of the book, Wolfe gives credit to the dozens of people who helped him "re-create the mental atmosphere of the subjective reality" of life with the Pranksters. He says, "All the events, details and dialogue I have recorded are either what I saw and heard myself or were told to me by people who were there themselves or were recorded on tapes or film or in writing."[5] Wolfe's book isn't just beautifully written. It's beautifully *researched* as well.

At the other extreme of the scale might be the CBS "60 Minutes" investigative team with its armada of cameras and microphones bursting into the office of some fly-by-night aluminum siding salesman. (Of course, they *want* to intimidate their quarry into blurting out revealing statements. They also want to impress the Great God Nielsen.) Less melodramatic and far more common are the growing number of technology addicts described here by distinguished journalist Gay Talese:

> I myself have been interviewed by writers carrying recorders, and as I sit answering questions, I see them half-listening, nodding pleasantly, and relaxing in the knowledge that the little wheels are rolling. But what they are getting from me . . . is not the insight that comes from deep probing and perceptive analysis and old-fashioned leg-work; it is rather the first-draft drift of my mind, a once-over-lightly dialogue that . . . too frequently reduces the once-artful craft of magazine writing to the level of talk radio on paper.[6]

Like a lot of freelance writers, I slide up and down the middle of the scale. Since most of my stories don't involve public figures who spend half of their lives talking into microphones, I often begin by simply chatting, not about the Very Important Topics on my mental checklist, but about whatever strikes me as truly interesting. I trust my own curiosity and enthusiasm, and I'm willing to go with the flow of the conversation. I figure that if I act natural, the person I'm talking to will, too. Eventually we'll get to the sensitive or heavy-duty stuff.

JON R. LUOMA
FREELANCE SCIENCE WRITER

"Get your facts first, and then you can distort them as much as you please." —Mark Twain.

As usual, Twain was just kidding around, because facts—carefully acquired, weighed, and rendered—form the foundation on which nonfiction is built. Get your facts wrong, and your apparently rock-solid story collapses fast. So may your reputation.

Few writers know this as well as Jon R. Luoma, author of books on difficult, complicated subjects like acid rain (*Troubled Skies, Troubled Waters,* Viking) and animal breeding in zoos (*A Crowded Ark,* Houghton-Mifflin). He also has written a substantial part of a leading high school biology textbook. A regular contributor to *The New York Times* science section and *Audubon,* the Minneapolis-based Luoma interviews botanists, chemists, or zoologists almost daily, yet he has little formal training in science (he majored in creative writing in college).

How does he cope? He'll often start by reading summary or overview articles, then quickly ask—"beg!"—one or a number of experts to hold his hand and walk him through the topic. "Sometimes I say, 'Imagine a friend of yours invited you to dinner and has a moderately bright 11-year-old who wants to know what you do. Tell him.' The key to it all is not to be embarrassed about your ignorance. Keep asking questions and don't be afraid to restate something in your own words to see if you have it right."

After the interview, Luoma will dig deeper into the literature, compile detailed notes on cards or in his computer, sort them, write some of the technical explanations, and then double-check anything he doesn't fully understand, often by reading a few paragraphs over the phone to his original source. "You have to accumulate much more material than will ever go into the story," he says. When he's finished with his manuscript, he prefers to have a "second party" go back and check his facts.

On national magazines, this process usually involves using a staff researcher or fact-checker, who will pore over statistics, check direct quotations, and double- and triple-check titles and proper nouns—assistance that is "especially helpful to me since I'm not good with

spelling people's names," says Luoma. For controversial statements of
fact (scientists argue as often as anyone else) the checker may call up
sources on all sides, plus contact an uninvolved third party.

"I work extremely hard to get my facts straight," says Luoma, "but
fact-checkers let freelance writers sleep a little easier."[7]

Interviewing

A few years ago I wrote a story about a high school English teacher
and basketball coach who dug graves on weekends. Tom Bridinger
had learned grave-digging from his father, a cemetery superinten-
dent, and was very serious about doing it "right," not with a fancy
backhoe but with an ordinary shovel. "After all," he told me, "digging
a grave is the last special thing you can do for someone."

One rainy Saturday morning, I interviewed him at work. Sitting
respectfully on a nearby tombstone while Tom rolled back damp sod
in strips like small carpets, I started off by asking him about sports.
In return, he asked me about basketball in New York, since I told him
I grew up there. Gradually I maneuvered the conversation to childhood generally, then to what it was like to grow up with a cemetery as
a playground. Answering between shovelfuls, Tom soon seemed to
forget that I was a reporter whom he didn't know particularly well.
Down and down into the ground he went, and deeper and deeper
into his past.

"Mind if I write that down?" I asked after a particularly revealing
answer. Out came my notebook with the list of questions I'd jotted
down over breakfast. By the time he'd dug his way down to knee-level,
he was yakking away and I was writing like mad. (No, I don't take
shorthand, but I've developed my own cryptic scrawl that I put into
full sentences the moment I'm alone. Through practice, I've also
developed an excellent though hardly Capote-esque short-term memory.) Here's a typical page of notes:

headstone — heads are always West

"This is therapy" (Ask more on
                      later !!)

I'm dating this girl from Texas now &
she said: "Honey, you don't really dig
graves, do you? That's not what you
wanna do the rest of your life, is
it?"
          I would, though....

DAD - 9th gr. ed. but grad from life
   summer cum laude
          "My brothers took over when Dad
     finished — or died."   (finished?)

Tom walks off 6 boot marks : "I used
to have to measure, but now I can just
step it off"   — puts in metal
pins like this → ♉

          7' 10" x 3' 2" then lays out string
  "but Dad taught me to eyeball it"
     _ "when you're close to the headstone
  it always freezes..."

In the gloom of that Saturday morning, Tom and I had ourselves a
fine old time. I even tried my hand at digging so he could show me
how his father taught him the tricks of the trade. Later, by phone, I
asked Tom to fill in a few things I was afraid I'd gotten garbled. In
the story I eventually published in *Ohio Magazine*, his voice became a
major element.

Not the only element, however. I wanted to write a story, not just a
string of quotations. And so *my* voice went into the writing, too, as I

observed, interpreted, cut, paraphrased and summarized what Tom said, as well as put some of it down verbatim.

How do you know when to quote and when not to? First, you rely on instinct and the skills acquired through writing and more writing. Second, you follow a rule of thumb that Gay Talese describes approximately like this (I can't seem to find where he said this, so I'll have to paraphrase):

> If you talk better than they do, do it.

Talese isn't referring to the Queen's English. By almost anyone's standards, Tom Bridinger is an articulate man, but when he spoke of the "art" of grave-digging, he was positively eloquent: "When I'm about to take that last shovelful of dirt, I always think of a sculptor getting ready to take the final chip off a statue—you know, the hammer poised over the tip of the nose or the chin." How could I improve on that? Into the story it went, just as he said it. Occasionally, he described something in ten sentences that I either had no room for or could say myself better in two, so I summarized or paraphrased and dropped the quotation marks.

JESSICA MITFORD
FROM "KIND" QUESTIONS TO "CRUEL"

If you need information from people who won't talk to you, or who will but, like human mine detectors, invariably steer away from explosive topics, go read Jessica Mitford's *Poison Penmanship: The Gentle Art of Muckraking*. This is the best, most readable primer I know for the investigative writer, although Mitford's methods are not for everyone.

Mitford wrote *The American Way of Death*, a 1963 exposé of deceptive practices in the funeral industry, and "Let Us Now Appraise Famous Writers," a savagely funny *Atlantic* investigation into the Famous Writers School and its "Guiding Faculty" which, she discovered, did far less "guiding" than advertised. *Poison Penmanship* contains all or parts of these and other muckraking pieces, plus detailed notes about how she got her facts.

She's especially good on interviewing "Unfriendly Witnesses," for whom she suggests a list of questions in ascending order from Kind to Cruel:

Kind questions are designed to lull your quarry into a conversational mood: 'How did you first get interested in funeral directing as a career?' 'Could you suggest any reading material that might help me to understand more about problems [of running prisons]?' and so on. By the time you get to the Cruel questions—'What is the wholesale cost of your casket retailing for three thousand dollars?' 'How do you justify censoring a prisoner's correspondence with his lawyer in violation of California law?'—your interlocutor will find it hard to duck and may blurt out a quotable nugget.[8]

Meanwhile, back at the Hall of Fame, as I listen to stories of train and motorcycle crashes and other totally insane, carefully orchestrated exploits, I begin to sink into one of my favorite reportorial modes—Hanging Out.

I Hang Out when I'm not sure what I really want out of a situation, which is most of the time. And so I try to temporarily erase my background research and walk in with the widest peripheral vision possible, as though it were my first day on the planet. It's something like this description of *New Yorker* writer John McPhee:

When McPhee conducts an interview he tries to be as blank as his notebook pages, totally devoid of preconceptions, equipped with only the most elementary knowledge. He has found that imagining he knows a subject is a disadvantage, for that prejudice will limit his freedom to ask, to learn, to be surprised by unfolding evidence. Since most stories are full of unsuspected complexity, an interviewer hardly needs to *feign* ignorance; the stronger temptation is to bluff with a show of knowledge or to trick the informant into providing simple, easily digestible answers. . . . [McPhee] would rather risk seeming ignorant to get a solid, knotty answer.[9]

These observations come from editor William L. Howarth's introduction to *The John McPhee Reader,* a sampling from twelve of McPhee's books. Howarth provides a satisfyingly thorough (if slightly idolatrous) portrait of the research-to-writing process of one of the best nonfiction writers going.

As more stunt artists arrive in Moab (there's an especially good turn-out because a long Hollywood writers' strike has created free time for performers—more "dumb luck" for me), I wander amiably around, eavesdropping or introducing myself to people and asking about whatever strikes me as interesting. Not bad for a guy who was once too shy to go to his senior prom—a debilitating diffidence that somehow, thank God, I have mostly outgrown.

Each night in my motel room I noodle a bit and go over my notes, filling in illegible gaps before I forget the context, writing questions for the next day, checking to see that the better monologues made it intact onto tape. I also circle compelling phrases—Jody: "Stunt talent's just a natural thing, and it's rare as chicken lips"—and I write down a few of my own impressions:

Stunt men all connoisseurs of gravity . . .

moab in early a-m. : nobody up but tumbleweed rolls bounces down middle of Main St.

Late in day, the red rocks actually seem to glow . . . - (may be use Ed. Abbey quote from Desert Solitaire? ?)

When I'm doing research, I usually dress to blend in. In Moab, I choose a variation on my standard professor garb of tweed coat and jeans. I wear a *t-shirt* and jeans. Pretty soon, no one pays much attention to my notebook and fast-moving pen, my little tape recorder, my pocket camera. I become just another character—as I have planned to do.

Photography

If you're adept at taking pictures—good for you. Your photos can help get your story published (for sometimes double the pay), especially if they record one-time ocurrences or illustrate something too remote for others to get to, say that grizzly bear rearing up in front of you on the slopes of Mt. Denali. It also helps if you're a Rembrandt with a camera, incapable of creating a poor image.

I happen to be capable of creating *plenty* of poor images, along with an occasional decent shot, and I'm not likely to get much better. I don't work at it; the technology annoys me, and I feel the camera changes my relationship with my subject, whether it's an ocean vista or a person standing in front of my nose. It somehow pushes me away.

Thus, one of the first things I do on a story is get the names and numbers of any photographers that I or an editor can contact later. Then I forget about them. If one comes with me on assignment, we often confer briefly beforehand about good shots, then go our separate ways. (Working for *Modern Maturity,* for example, the photographer might concentrate on the older stuntmen.) If the editor is planning to send a photographer later, as was the case in my grave-digging story, I'll pass on some ideas for good shots.

So I use my automatic camera only sparingly, mostly to remind myself later about odd little details: the number of eagles embroidered on a cowboy's shirt, the color of the swerving car that a stuntman leaps from onto hard, hard asphalt, the exact bend of the knees as John Hagner prepares to dive off a roof.

On the second day of the festival, a man named Richard Fraga actually *does* jump out of a car. When he tells John Hagner he'll be happy to liven up the show by "jumping out of a speeding car or something," and Hagner says, "Well, you'd have to do it in an asphalt parking lot," Fraga shrugs: "Makes no difference to me." When Fraga doesn't do this sort of thing for movies or TV commercials, he runs a school for aspiring stunt artists in California.

Fraga intrigues me. He's about my height and build, about my age. After I've talked with him a while, I think I see a glimpse of one of my earlier selves: the youngster who would climb to the top of a swaying, forty-foot maple tree and casually wave to gaping playmates. What's happened to that kid who flaunted recklessness like a wind-snapped banner? What happens to that kid in all of us? I jot down these and similar questions, things that didn't occur to me a few days ago. And I begin to wonder . . .

Soon I fill one notebook (writing on only one side of each page to avoid later confusion and endless page flipping). Then I fill another with notes about the parade, induction ceremony, and ribbon breaking that closes the festival. In all, I scribble down dozens of conversations and hundreds of details.

Like this page from my notebook:

stunt 6/88

Jim Babcock (stuntman — Gunsmoke, Bonanza)
   — started "ridin' rodeo," grew up Port Angeles, Wash., did horse tricks for other kids, fell off, etc. . . . .

Heroes : John Wayne
          Yak Canutt (created
safety equip for stuntmen, like
"step stirrups" ⌐ that wouldn't
catch your foot

J B says that in old "Rin Tin Tin" TV
show he'd play an Indian, ride one way,
then everybody wipe off war paint, put
on Calvary uniforms + charge back across
cameras the other way !! Saved $$

Can I possibly use all this . . . STUFF?

Of course not, even though I'm pretty sure by now that this isn't going to be a normal "feature story" or something easy to pin down very quickly. As I said before, I tend to over-research. But I usually find that my cramped fingers, blurry eyes, and messy desk are small sacrifices for the advantages of having a sea of facts to choose from later. It sounds almost biblical: the wider the net you cast, the more big fish you'll catch.

As I drive back to Colorado, I realize that I've caught a lot of big fish. But I haven't yet separated them from the smaller ones.

That will come in the writing.

Chapter 4

Getting It Done

Writing and Re-writing and Re-writing and . . .

OKAY, LET'S GET down to the business of writing, or what an old journalism professor of mine called "pushing a noun against a verb without having an accident."

As soon as I'm back home in Colorado, my stunt knowledge at high tide, I start in on a kind of Grand Shuffle. This is my own quirkily developed version of the focusing that most writers do. At this point in the creative process, some writers laboriously type out everything they've jotted down or recorded on tape; I tend to pore over and arrange and rearrange my notes, including my original background research. Usually it helps me find an "organizing principle" for my story and a place to start writing, a place to *work my way in* through all the material I've gathered—observations, interviews, books, off-the-wall ideas.

But what *is* my story, anyway?

Based on just a glance at my bulging manila folder marked "Stunt," some limited topics quickly suggest themselves. Here are a few, including my initial reactions:

John Hagner Profile (Lots of information.)
Hall of Fame Feature (*Museum Magazine*? *Smithsonian* if I'm ambitious.)

Insurance/Law Suits (But probably not my kind of topic—too much legal stuff.)

Training School (Not now, but in the future I could visit Fraga's "School of Hard Knocks" for, say, *TV Guide.*)

Old Guys Profile (Hagner, Goodrich, Whitey, Iron Eyes—try *Modern Maturity* or *Golden Years.*)

Moab Movie Mecca (John Ford and others filmed there.)

Stunts vs. Real World Violence (Do Rambo toys affect kids? Do I have an opinion?)

Personal Memoir (I used to think just the way the stunt artists did as kids. What happened?)

Some of these topics, or maybe some combination of them, are starting to look interesting. But I still don't quite know what I want.

So I flip again through my dusty, burrito-stained notebooks (I found a good Mexican restaurant in Moab), and I start to highlight interesting phrases and observations with a yellow magic marker. Soon I'm drawing arrows to trace connections that are only now becoming clear to me, and writing new ideas in the margins. For example:

MOAB
6/25

Hagner brings up Iron Eyes for prayer
JH — "220 footprints here — more than
Graumann's Chinese Theatre" — (odd
✱ to have people stuck ~~in cement~~ when
action is their forte)

JH starts by balancing a sword, then
Iron Eyes' cane (on chin), deer antlers,
(stops & says: "I need a Kirk Douglas
chin" - haha), Randy's walker,
coat rack (brass), 4 ft-long fish,
banjo

Odd: Work in
theme of
Grquuolednus
vs.
Flight? Heavuns vs. Lightruns ??

Bert — "I think this is the best
        day of my life. Mae West en-
couraged me in my singing" (C starts
on song

✱   ✱

＝stunt men are Actors in the
    Sky, they.
                                    ✱
                        \ great
                        Title ?? phrase!

Certainly I'll write about John Hagner and some of the others, but the more I mull it over, the more "I"—me, John Calderazzo—begins to crowd into the story. The question is, do I really belong? Will I clutter it up? I'm often annoyed at authors who insist on injecting themselves into *everything* they write—subjectivity gone wild. How will this affect the structure of the piece?

Finding the Right Structure

I go outside for a long, solitary walk, searching for these answers—and an organizing principle. An organizing principle is the bone structure on which the flesh of the story hangs, and none too flabbily if everything works out. Some organizing principles are imposed, usually by institutions, and some, like the one I hope (Please!) to stumble upon soon, arise organically from the material.

Imposed Structure

To explain further: the famous "inverted pyramid" structure of most news stories is a "Just the facts, Ma'am" formula imposed by practically every daily newspaper in the country. For the sake of efficiency, objectivity (although writing is of course never 100 percent objective), and hurried readers, the most important facts appear unadorned with adverbs and adjectives at the top of the story, as in the news blip I did for *USA TODAY.* Or as in this story from the June 13, 1989, final edition of the *Denver Post:*

CHINESE CONSULATES FILM U.S. PROTESTS

Chinese consulates in New York and San Francisco have been photographing and compiling blacklists of participants in U.S. demonstrations favoring the Beijing democratic movement, Chinese student leaders say.

At a demonstration in San Francisco immediately after the Tiananmen Square massacre, student protestors saw Chinese Consulate staff holding video and still cameras on the roof and at the windows of the Chinese Consulate.

In New York, consular staff were seen with cameras in the windows during . . .

And so on. Another imposed structure is the so-called Five Paragraph Theme taught with numbing regularity in many high school and college composition courses. You probably know it all too well:

I   Introduction
       Thesis: "There are three reasons why the Five Paragraph Theme should be banned from the planet."
II   "One, it's impossibly simplistic."
III   "Two, it assumes all subjects/problems can be divided into three main points."
IV   "Three, it offers the writer all the freedom of an iron lung."
V   Conclusion

Of course, there are many variations on all of these. Newspapers, for instance, offer news analysis stories, editorials, columns, etc. Daily feature stories give the writer a bit more room and a wider choice of approaches. Big, well-illustrated Sunday supplement stories usually offer the most freedom of all, the greatest opportunity for a newspaper writer to use an idiosyncratic voice and a structure that breaks from formula; but they're a dying breed, often the first victims of financial belt-tightening at big-city newspapers. And, fortunately, not all comp teachers insist on dividing reality into three neat slices and 500 words.

Organic Structure

How does a structure "arise organically" (like whole-grain bread?) from the material?

Let's go back to the grave for this one—to the grave Tom Bridinger was working on when I interviewed him on that rainy Saturday morning. By the time Tom finished his "sculpting," I knew that I had the organizing principle for my story. I would simply describe the digging of one grave, from the moment Tom sliced through the damp green sod until he hauled himself out of that meticulously wrought hole. Along the way, I would let Tom (or myself, when I could do it "better") talk about what it meant to him, how he grew up playing in the cemetery, and so forth. This excerpt is typical:

Tom works on the third and final layer, sparks shooting up as he grazes a rock while squaring a corner. He's got his rhythm now and digs hard, sensing the end. "I'd like to get my jogs in before nightfall," he says. The mist has lifted, but the air still feels as wet as the clay that squishes around his feet.

"These people that buy $12,000 copper vaults while there are kids starving all over the world—I can't see it. We're gonna go back to dust anyway. Me, I'll be cremated. I'll have them put my ashes right next to Dad. Or right on top."

He's near the bottom now. A few worms wriggle out of the walls and drop to the heavy clay . . .

I felt lucky. It's rare that an organizing principle comes to me so quickly or fits the story so well. After only a week of writing every morning and part of a few afternoons, I mailed an eleven-page double-spaced (about 3000-word) story to *Ohio Magazine*, which accepted it immediately.

The stunt artists, however, are proving elusive. About halfway through my long walk, I begin composing a very shaky "lead," a description of the dramatic moment that actually opened the Hall of Fame. (Luckily, I live in the country, so there aren't many people around to point at the silly man talking to himself.) Here's what I come up with:

In Moab, Utah, the summer sun smashes me into the ground. I stand in a crowd, squint, and watch a 60-year-old man in a red cape and "Captain Action" sweatshirt teeter 30 feet up on the ledge of a converted Mormon church. His name is John Hagner. Not far from where I stand, two of John's friends have stretched a ribbon above two piled-up air mattresses. When John crashes through it, three days of festivities will end and the Hollywood Stuntmen's Hall of Fame will officially open for business.

Not bad: it's a scene with dramatic tension (What'll happen when he jumps?) and interesting contrasts (a 60-year-old acting like a kid). But I don't know where to go next. However, the longer I walk, the more a couple of other passages from my notes start to circulate in my brain—a good sign. When I get back to my desk, I look them up, turn on my faithful word-cruncher (the three-year-old, no frills computer on which I know how to do nothing at all but write sentences and format paragraphs), and type them in, pretty much as I first jotted them down.

Fraga/other stunt guys' fascination w/ childhood movies is like mine—reminds me of why I liked figuring stunt stuff when a kid (Tarzan,

Ivanhoe, Vikings)—the way I'd concoct long slow-mo fight fantasies in Jr
Hi Engl class, me rescuing the teacher (Miss ??—well, she was pretty)
from thug-types older than me after school . . .

OR . . .

How when I was young I'd spend long hrs on summer eves when world
was limitless & my barefeet flew on grass (damp deepdeep green of
backyard)—& practice getting shot off make-believe horse or falling out
of tree (like Hagner did for his friends) . . . or something like this . . .

These are rough, but give off a few sparks, I think. The "damp
deepdeep green" of the backyard grass hints at childhood as a Garden
of Eden, a world that seemed "limitless"—not exactly an original or
earth-shaking thought, but something that feels meaningful to *me*.
Both paragraphs also have the potential to become vignettes or scenes
in a story. After all, as long as you get your facts straight, you can
write a dramatic scene or portray a character every bit as vividly in
nonfiction as in a novel or short story. (Though I minored in journalism in college, the course that taught me the most about nonfiction
writing was a fiction workshop.)

Next, I plunge into a kind of research that isn't often talked about—
the research of memoir, of self, in which I wander through what you
might call the book stacks of my own past. I *become* my own library.
Fortunately, a lot of the "books" are still on the shelves, so it doesn't
take long to write out this draft:

When I was in seventh grade study hall, while some of my classmates
actually did their homework, I daydreamed about rescuing my only
pretty teacher—whose name I've long forgotten—from ninth grade
thugs, the kind who curled a fist under my chin and sneered, "Hey,
punk, you wanna spit chiclets?" One by one, I beat them up. My reward
was a kiss on top of the head.

I look it over a few times. It *stinks*. The opening sentence takes
practically the whole paragraph—much too long, even though I know
wordiness and a crawling pace are some of the many things that rewriting remedies. Worse, the "scene" has little setting or plot, and the
characters, including the pre-adolescent me, bore me. The phrase
"some of my classmates actually did their homework" seems to indicate that I didn't, or that I routinely took a very cavalier attitude
toward schoolwork. That simply isn't true (I was cavalier only *some* of
the time), and so the sentence comes off as macho posturing; it's a bit

phony. Finally, the entire scene seems a long way from the subject of stunt artists. If I was tapping away on my old typewriter, I would rip out the page, ball it up, and sky-hook it into the wastebasket, a visceral pleasure I miss on the computer.

Oh well, these are the breaks of the writing life. When I was younger and thought that literature flowed in unbroken, beautiful sentences from every writer's pen, I might have walked away from the desk, brooding about the futility of it all. But that was before experience showed me how concentrated doses of time and energy could help me "break through" if I just kept believing in myself and in my material. (Which proves, I guess, that not everything about growing older is bad.)

A writer friend calls this the Chipping at Stone stage of writing. I often console myself with the knowledge that even the most famous writers face it occasionally. In a recent installment of his memoirs, Philip Roth says that when he starts a novel he sometimes writes 100 pages of lifeless prose before he finds even a single paragraph worth saving. And here's Annie Dillard on the daunting problem of finding structure:

> Every book has an intrinsic impossibility, which its writer discovers as soon as his first excitement dwindles. The problem is structural; it is insoluble; it is why no one can ever write this book. Complex stories, essays and poems have this problem, too—the prohibitive structural defect the writer wishes he never noticed. He writes it in spite of that. He finds ways to minimize the difficulty; he strengthens other virtues; he cantilevers the whole narrative out into thin air and it holds.[10]

So who am I to complain after only a few crummy sentences? Here, then, is my next, somewhat cantilevered effort, which takes slightly longer:

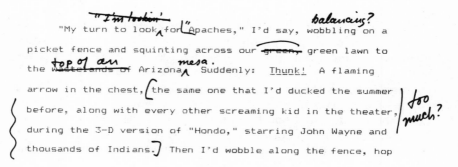

"My turn to look for Apaches," I'd say, wobbling on a picket fence and squinting across our green green lawn to the top of an Arizona mesa. Suddenly: Thunk! A flaming arrow in the chest, the same one that I'd ducked the summer before, along with every other screaming kid in the theater, during the 3-D version of "Hondo," starring John Wayne and thousands of Indians. Then I'd wobble along the fence, hop *too alliterative ??*

speed
up
speed up!

```
down (making sure not to catch my(pants on the(pickets),

roll a while (depending on how wet the grass was), fling out
                                          ugh!
my arms, gurgle, and, to a smattering of applause, die.

    Or, zapped by Ming the Merciless, Emperor of Mongo and
                                                       careful
king of the late afternoon TV reruns, I'd drop branch by

branch through my favorite tree like a human Slinky, groan-

ing all the way.

    Every night we died at the hands of Robin Hood, Flash

Gordon, Tarzan, Errol Flynn, Buster Crabbe, Johnny Weismul-

ler, and nobody ever got hurt . . .
```

I don't like this, either. It's unfocused, stilted, overlong (I can already see the reader yawning) and too stuffed with me, me, me. Who cares about my stupid childhood fantasies, anyway?

Well, to be honest, *I* do. And as you can see from the filigree of editing that I added the moment I printed out the passage, I suspect that I have something here worth working on, despite its weaknesses.

You may wonder why I didn't edit this on the computer, aside from the fact that blipping the original to electronic oblivion would have left no record for the writing of this book. Most of the time, I do make my changes on the machine. One of its great strengths is to speed up rewriting. But now and then, I like to unplug myself from the vast energy network humming along in my wall and just go sit under a tree with a pen and piece of paper—one of the many acts of independence that make writing so attractive.

Okay, take a minute now and reread this second try. Despite the clunkiness, a few things show promise. First, the concrete details ("Hondo," Errol Flynn) pile up quickly, a sign that I've gone deeper into myself than in the frivolous save-the-teacher daydream. Second, the connection between my own fantasy life and the illusions created by Hollywood seem to arise more naturally out of the material. Third, the reference to my early sense of caution (checking my pants legs before I jumped) has taken me by surprise. This certainly seems worth exploring. Is writing really the process of discovery that English teachers always say it is? Yes.

Notice also a few of my changes.

Reducing "My turn to look for Apaches" to "Apaches" cuts needless words, de-emphasizes me, and punches up the all-important opening line.

An "Arizona mesa" is more specific than "wastelands" and therefore easier to imagine, especially if I want to create a camera's-eye image of Indians silhouetted neatly and unrealistically on the horizon—a staple shot in "B" westerns that also saves the producer from having to hire too many extras.

A "smattering of applause" is a cliché, pure and simple. ("Pure and simple" is also a cliché, but I'll leave it in for the benefit of this little joke.)

On the other hand, a "human Slinky" is novel—too novel, I quickly decide. It parades its own cleverness. Besides, "dropping branch by careful branch" gets the job done without it.

Even with the changes, this draft still needs lots of work. The tone especially seems out of control; I know I can do better. I wonder if a dreamier, less slangy beginning might improve it—something like "It was a great summer to take a punch to the chin . . ."

It was a good summer to take a punch on the chin or a bullet in the stomach. Our backyard grass was damp and soft, and the warm nights were so full of lightning bugs that even without a moon my playmates and I could watch each other, in a kind of slow motion, crash through windows, fall from horses, and fall into moats. We were the stars of the late-afternoon reruns: Flash and Dale and Ming the Merciless, Tarzan and Sheena and Clyde Beatty, Robin and his Merry Men.

"Apaches," I'd say, balancing on the crossbeam of a picket fence and squinting across my parents' green Long Island lawn to an Arizona mesa, where hundreds of Indians had silhouetted themselves against a technicolor sky. Suddenly, *Thunk!* An arrow in the chest. Then I'd wobble along the fence, hop down (making sure not to hook my sneaker laces), stagger, roll, fling out my arms, and die.

Night after night we got kicked, shot, stabbed and blown up, and we never got hurt. But then, our world was better padded than most. Even in real fights, the kids in my neighborhood rarely punched for the face; and years later Vietnam took mostly those who lived on the other side of town.

This isn't about to earn me the Pulitzer Prize, but it's getting better. I'm even beginning to like it. As I read it over I feel myself falling back into the cocoon of innocence I grew up in, a sublime ignorance of the ways of the world. Soon more memories come flooding in—so many, in fact, that I'm practically wallowing in nostalgia. I've got to be careful here. Nostalgia is one byproduct of personal reflection that I distrust. It makes me think of the drunken sentiments that burble forth at high school reunions: "Wow, weren't *those* the days?" No, not really.

There are other problems, as my editing marks again indicate.

In my first paragraph, "fall from horses" and "fall into moats" are lazy and repetitive, using the lowest common denominator of verb. Finding more concrete, interesting, and precise words is usually just a matter of thinking for a minute or reaching for the thesaurus next to my desk. (Mark Twain once said that "the difference between the almost-right word and the right word is really a large matter. 'Tis the difference between the lightning bug and the lightning.") "Flash and Dale" is probably too cryptic a description of Flash Gordon and his endlessly imperiled girlfriend Dale Arden; a reader who doesn't already know them might quit right there; a possibly obscure reference that appears at the start of a story, before the reader is swept along by the narrative, can be dangerous. "Robin and his Merry Men" is a cliché; "Robin Hood" is cleaner.

"*Thunk!* An arrow in the chest." Oh, please! This and the mock death scene that follows strike me as embarrassingly long and melodramatic, or too slapstick for the mood that is starting to take over the opening—even if I really did act out those things when I was young. This section is a strong candidate for the writer's dump heap, that gargantuan pile of not-always-badly-written phrases and sentences that just happen to be born in the wrong time and place. After all, what you take out of a piece of writing is just as important as what you put in.

The last paragraph really needs bashing around. There are language problems: two uses of "got" ("got kicked," "got hurt") in the same short sentence emphasizes the blunt tone of this sometimes ungraceful verb form—a tone that clashes for no good reason with semi-poetic, slightly precious phrases like "our world was better padded than most" and "Vietnam took mostly those . . ." It's as though two very different writers are at work. Obviously I haven't yet found my voice for this piece.

There are also philosophical and structural problems. By introducing real wars like Vietnam so early in the story, I'm at least subtly leading the reader to expect further consideration of "big" themes like the effect of childhood cowboy and Indian games on adult violence. If you'd like to read a thoughtful examination of this serious topic, take a look at Scott Russell Sanders' "Death Games" in *A Paradise of Bombs,* his very fine collection of essays. But I'm not at all sure what *I* think of the issue.

Nevertheless, I can't just dismiss the topic. Words and actions are rife with political ramifications, and the very concept of the stunt artist—an expert at creating the illusion of violence for millions of people—quite naturally brings up the subject. Even though I'm interested in John Wayne primarily as a movie star and cultural icon, his name is synonymous with the kind of simplistic "Rambo" politics I hate. So I have to address this problem somehow and yet keep the story from veering into a thicket I'm not prepared to write my way out of. On top of it all, I've got to get the narrative back to Moab and the Hall of Fame, the place that prompted all this soul-searching.

Off I go on another long walk (my favorite way to write, and *not* write) to think hard about my youthful fantasies. They really *don't* have much to do with real-world violence, I decide, unless of course I'm as blind as poor Oedipus to the forces that have shaped me. I also think about my younger self's emerging sense of physical danger (the "pants legs" that I've rewritten as the more specific and more accurate "sneaker laces"). Maybe I should try to evoke a slightly earlier, more naive stage of childhood.

Now, if you can possibly keep all of the above in mind, bear with me for a look at this new version of the story's opening lines:

> It was a good summer to take a punch on the chin or a bullet in the gut. Our backyard grass was soft, and the warm, windless nights were so full of lightning bugs that even without a moon my friends and I could take turns, in flickering slow motion, crashing through windows, exploding from foxholes, and tumbling into moats. It had nothing to do with real violence—the kind I'd seen in the schoolyard or on the Friday night fights I watched with my father—and so we died as we pleased, the falling stars of old movies and TV reruns: Flash Gordon, Dr. Zarkov and Ming the Merciless, Tarzan, Sheena, Clyde Beatty, and anybody played by Errol Flynn.
>
> I was the most serious of the bunch. Small and agile, I'd swing through my favorite maple tree or somersault into piles of rotting, sweet-smelling grass. "Apaches," I'd say, climbing onto a picket fence and squinting across our Long Island lawn to an Arizona mesa, where thousands of Indians had silhouetted themselves against a technicolor sky—a sure sign of attack. Then, with a yell, I'd leap. To move in the air was to fly, to float in the endless space of my imagination. And I gave barely a thought to the earth that was rushing up to meet me.

Summer, many years later. While the sun smashes me into the baked ground of Moab, Utah, I stand in a crowd and squint up at sixty-year-old John Hagner, in a red cape and a sweatshirt that says "Captain Action," teetering thirty feet above me on the ledge of a converted Mormon church. Nearby, two of John's friends hold a ribbon above two piled-up air mattresses. When John crashes through the ribbon, three days of festivities will end, and the Hollywood Stuntmen's Hall of Fame will open for business.

Smoother all around, I think. (Ambitious, too. It looks like I'm in for a long haul.) And the third paragraph, yoking those gauzy summer evenings of the past with the sun-baked harshness of the present, provides a dramatic tension that wasn't there before.

But then, the writing *should* be much better. I've redone this thing about ten times: the drafts I've included here are only highlights of the laborious rewriting process. Ferocious rewriting is a habit I share with many writers, and computers only help us indulge the obsession. It's said that Dylan Thomas wrote the wildly lyrical "Fern Hill" 125 times. (What would he have done with a computer? Hocked it at the nearest pub?)

Does all this rewriting become a drudgery? Nope, at least not to me. In fact, watching your work get incrementally better—with an occasional and always surprising Great Leap Forward—is one of the greatest satisfactions of the writing life, or of any creative life.

Of course, not everyone fanatically refines and polishes the way I do before inching forward. On certain rare and miraculous occasions (even for me) the sentences click almost from the first few minutes you sit down to write, although you'd better not count on this. And many writers plow their way through most or all of a first draft before sitting back and blinking over what they've wrought. This, or something like it, may work best for you. I have a good friend, a professional writer, who simply sits, carefully reads his notes, outlines and composes in his head, then types out a couple of pages that are 99 percent final drafts. He has written more than a dozen nonfiction books, and his style is as clear as a glass of water. Sometimes I hate him.

But my method is more than just obsessive. The opening section of any good story, fiction or nonfiction, contains all or most of the important elements that gradually become obvious in the telling of the tale. So when I'm working and reworking those first few paragraphs, I'm also laying the foundation for everything that's to come:

each phrase and sentence ripples forward with implications for the rest of the narrative. Eventually, I begin to see a rough outline—the outline that a lot of writers create before they put down a word.

According to the way it's shaping up, the story now seems to contain these major elements:

John Hagner
me
events I saw in Moab
the world of stunt artists generally

That's a lot of elements, especially when they're all still vying for top billing. And if the barroom brawl inside my head isn't bad enough, there's the imposing mass of my research. I've interviewed more than a dozen stunt artists and taken notes on scores of little incidents in Moab.

Yes, yes, yes, I know my story might be simpler if I just stick to one easy-to-grasp topic, and if I was really pressed for time or money I might cave in and knock off some standard feature articles on a couple of the ideas I listed at the start of this chapter. But there's something really niggling at me here, something complicated that I can't yet find words for, and I want to discover it.

Besides, why not write as if I were "dying," as Annie Dillard urges? Why not write exactly what I want, the way I want, the first time through? This is when my excitement and curiosity about the material are freshest, and this is what the hard-earned independence of the freelancer is all about. I can always write a different version—aim it at a "market" (see chapter seven)—later on.

Okay, I'm pleased enough by now with my opening paragraphs. Next, I'll sketch out events in approximately the order they occurred in Moab. A rough list of the highlights:

Thurs.
1) Stunt artists trickle in, meet, swap stories
2) Hagner practices saloon fight w/local group of stunt artists-in-training
3) I meet Fraga, take test that he gives to prospective students at his school in Cal.

Fri.
1) Fraga & Jody prepare Moab mayor's car for stunt demo
2) Fraga leaps from car in front of big crowd

Sat.
    1) Big parade led by trick roper Monty Montana, who later ropes spectators outside H of F
    2) Induction ceremony (JH jokes, Iron Eyes gives Indian prayer, Bert sings about stuntmen)
    3) JH leaps from roof to break ribbon to officially open the H of F

Oh boy, I've got to be careful here. This story is loaded with events and "scenes," overflows with colorful characters, and takes place over three days. That's a lot to keep straight, not even counting events from John Hagner's life, relevant historical moments in the stunt profession, and whatever I put in about myself. Plus my hard-earned, much-rewritten opening paragraphs which turn this chronology all around: I've started with a memoir of childhood, then jumped instantly to the *last* event of the Moab festival. If I don't rein in my material pretty soon, this story will take me for a long, unruly ride and buck off even the most dogged reader. Unless, that is, I want to write a book. But this doesn't feel like a book.

What to do?

Put down my head and write. Write, I hope, a little faster than before.

I start with the scenes I just listed above, the Utah chronology: Thursday #1, Thursday #2, etc. As I write, some of these episodes jump to life on the page with the first sentence, some start slowly but soon gather speed, and a few, despite all my efforts, barely limp along—onto the writer's junk heap they go, like dead batteries. The more I write about Moab and the stunt artists—these "connoisseurs of gravity," these "actors in the sky"—the more connections I start making with my own more earthbound, more conventional life.

Soon enough I have a "JC" list of items, examples of my own "heaviness" that counterpoints the "lightness" of stunt artists (and the illusion of lightness and grace that they create for the ordinary mortals who portray movie heroes). I might try weaving some of these into the Moab narrative. For instance:

- my inability to dance ("letting go," being "light" on my feet)
- my choice of high jumping (flight) as a high school sports obsession
- my choice of stuntmen as a story idea, especially with so many

other topics to choose from (boredom is NOT one of my life's problems)

And so now I try writing some of these personal vignettes. I write and I write. I write on the computer (I wonder: Shakespeare, Milton, the Brontë sisters, and Faulkner seemed to manage without one). I write in longhand on yellow legal pads, the way I did when I started scratching out poems and short stories in my senior year of college. (Like more than half the writers I know, I first majored in something that seemed far different from writing—in my case, physics and engineering.) And I write knowing that, even at this stage in the project, most of my sentences are destined for the dump heap, not necessarily because they're bad, but because they ultimately won't fit in. (More on this in a postscript to the story.) Along the way I also call John Hagner with an occasional question or check my growing collection of library books and magazine articles.

When I'm done, I have 40-plus decently written double-spaced pages of material I think are interesting and worthwhile. But they don't add up to a *story*, and there's still too much material. Let's face it, despite my seriousness about the material, I'm not writing *War and Peace* here, and I don't think I can ask a reader who's probably not much of a stunt fan to plow through all these pages. (Unless I'm writing on assignment for a publication with a well-defined audience, I usually figure I'm writing for intelligent, articulate readers who probably DON'T initially agree with me or share my enthusiasms. Preaching to the unconverted keeps writers lean, mean, and honest.)

So now it's time to cut, tighten the focus, pick up the pace. For this I need scissors, Scotch tape, Magic Marker, and a very large desk, such as the one in my office at Colorado State. I lay out all the pages on the desk (and on an adjoining table from which I clear piles of books and magazines). Next, I stand back from the whole mess and start highlighting and crossing out, snipping and taping, shuffling and reshuffling, weaving into the narration of the three-day festival strands of my own memories, John Hagner's, Jody's, history lessons of the profession, and God knows what else . . .

A typical page:

In junior high school,

eventually, of course

? Eventually, Reality intervened. First it came in the form
of gravity. I took up high jumping and won my first meet, but
during the rest of the season--and over the next few years--my
competitors all somehow turned into beanpoles, and the arc of my
own brief flights seemed to get flatter and flatter. I began to
sense that I'd have to look elsewhere, beyond the realm of the
corporal, to really fly.

Expand?

Meanwhile, my artistic tastes were changing: I abandoned
uncomplicated swashbucklers for a fling with film--grim, sub-
titled ruminations on life, usually in Sweden or rainy Paris, in
which nobody ever fell off a horse. Then, my father's war
stories--the kind of "Humor in Uniform" stuff run by Reader's
Digest--began to darken. And finally one night he and I sat in
front of the TV and watched a boxer again and again bludgeon
another man who was slumped helplessly on the ropes. Then, in
ferocious slow motion, the punches came again. The man, Benny
"Kid" Paret, never got up. Instantly different from the thousands of fake deaths I'd seen, this brutality wiped out the
of my ... the slick logic of violence. Nothing I've
seen in the twenty-five years since then has changed my mind.

out?

PROBLEM

Today's slash and crash movies make the old shoot-em-ups
look like stately quotations from Henry James; and I haven't sat
through a western, or heard enough, though, I
still find myself intrigued by the choreography of disaster, or
at least by the men and women who have made careers out of the
kind of fantasies I was once had, the fine athletes who give life
to illusion by acting for other actors on the most exhilarating
and unforgiving of stages: thin air.

my brains on slow ...

PRESENT TENSE

I think that's why I went to Moab, Utah a few weeks ago
and stood in a crowd, under a brilliant sun, while a man in a red
cape and a "Captain Action" sweatshirt teetered thirty feet up on
the ledge of a converted Mormon church. His name was John Hagner, and he was the founder of the Hollywood Stuntmen's Hall of
Fame and Museum. He in true stuntmen fashion, he was about to cut
the
four-day festival that marked the museum's grand opening.

Why was I standing in a crowd man?

Why did I ...

Down below, not far from where I stood, two of John's
friends held a ribbon above two piled-up air mattresses, the kind
that pole vaulters fall into. Another friend--Lee Aaker, a
veteran stuntman who once played the boy on television's "Rin Tin
Tin" (my favorite show until "Davey Crockett" taught me the true
meaning of idolatry)--carefully took a bead on John with a shotgun. Then he fired. John clutched his chest and staggered along
the ledge, swayed for a moment like a freshly cut pine, and
finally, red cape fanning out behind, tipped forward into space.

my high-jump I care...

I haven't exercised, dieted in...

more here??

'Don't move," said Richard Fraga, standing almost nose to
nose with me and looking very intense, though odd, in a ten
gallon hat, t-shirt, shorts and cowboy boots. "Movie-quality

Keep This

After a while the office is a wreck, and I know that the organizing principle for this story isn't going to leap out at me like sudden love. Well, once again, those are the breaks. Things are tough all over.

Snip, tape, shuffle, shuffle again.

What do you know? As the office gets messier and messier, my mind begins to clear, as though all of that interior clutter has poured out into the room, which is beginning to fill. The good ideas remain on the desk; the half-formed and inappropriate ones fall to the floor. Gradually an organizing principle is emerging for this ornery story. Finally, it's starting to take shape! The outline, which I never actually write out, evolves something like this:

```
          B.S. OUTLINE (BEFORE SHUFFLING)


Moab Events

     Thurs:   Stuntmen swap stories

              Fraga shows me how to "punch"

              Hagner practices brawl w/ locals

              Summary of who's who at festival

     Fri:     I take stunt test

              Fraga jumps from speeding car

     Sat:     Parade

              Induction ceremony

              Hagner jumps from roof


Background Information

     Hagner's past (his obsessiion)

     Moab description (beauty & remoteness)
```

    Precautions of stunt artists

    Jody McQueen accident, despite precautions

    History of profession (H of F mural)

    Yakima Canutt (real thing vs. movie actors)

My Personal Stuff

    Why have I come to Moab?

    5th grade, skip a stunt that badly injures Tommy

    Jr Hi, see a great athlete, eventually realize
        limits (painful) of my physical abilities

    Problems w/ dancing (vs. "natural grace" of stuntmen)

    I realize why I've come to Moab

Already-written opening scenes:

M.S. OUTLINE (MID-SHUFFLE)

1) *my playing at stunts as child*
2) *Hagner jumps from roof*

Moab Events

Thurs: Stuntmen swap stories *(break up & work in where appropriate)*

Fraga shows me how to "punch"

Hagner practices brawl w/ locals

Summary of who's who at festival

Fri: I take stunt test

Fraga jumps from speeding car

Sat: Parade

Induction ceremony

Hagner jumps from roof *(picks up P.1)*

✳ ⟨   ⟩ ✳   THE END

Background Information

Hagner's past (his obsessiion)

Moab description (beauty & remoteness)

Precautions of stunt artists

Jody McQueen accident, despite precautions

History of profession (H of F mural)

Yakima Canutt (real thing vs. movie actors)

My Personal Stuff

Why have I come to Moab?

5th grade, skip a stunt that badly injures Tommy

Jr Hi, see a great athlete, eventually realize
    limits (painful) of my physical abilities

Problems w/ dancing (vs. "natural grace" of stuntmen)

✳ ⟨ I realize why I've come to Moab ⟩ ✳

A.S. OUTLINE   (After Shuffling)

Original Lead

    It was a good summer to take a punch on the chin . . .

    Hagner jumps from roof

Complication of My Involvement

    Hagner's past (much like mine)

    Moab as remote destination

    Why have I come?

Unrolling of Narrative (mostly first day's events)

    Fraga shows me how to punch; Hagner brawls w/ friends

    Show precautions stunt artists use; tell Jody's

        accident story; jump to my near miss

More Narrative (mostly second day)

    See mural in Hall that depicts stunt history in U.S.

    Yak Canutt

    Me unable to dance (Clark Gable too!)

    Who's who of guests

    Fraga gives me stunt test (its difficulty reminds me of

        my first glimpse of a great "natural" athlete)

Rising Action (Physical & Otherwise) and Conclusion

    Fraga jumps from car

    Parade, then induction ceremony

    Hagner jumps from roof, really making me think

    RESOLUTION: I KNOW why I've come to Moab

With this organizing principle in mind, I go through a final shuffling of scenes and expository passages, rewrite or cut transitions, compress here, expand there, diddle around with the computer. Mostly, though, I cut. I know too much; I think I really have over-researched this time. Out goes Jody McQueen's beautiful and funny story about the stunt crew being mistaken for plotting criminals. As much as I like it, it simply doesn't fit into the story that's developing. (All the more reason to have put it in this book; it's not wasted after all.)

Gradually—after lots of sweat, grief, doubt, and the unparalleled exhilaration of creating something I care deeply for—out comes the 20-page story that you're about to see, the story that I've decided to call, after ex-Mr. America Bert Goodrich's song, "Actors in the Sky."

Chapter 5

Actors in the Sky

IT WAS A GOOD summer to take a punch on the chin or an arrow in the chest. Our backyard grass was soft, and the warm, windless nights were so full of lightning bugs that even without a moon my friends and I could take turns, in flickering slow motion, crashing through windows, exploding from foxholes, and tumbling into moats. It had nothing to do with real violence—the kind I'd seen in the schoolyard or on the Friday night fights I watched with my father—and so we died as we pleased, the falling stars of old movies and TV reruns: Flash Gordon, Dr. Zarkov and Ming the Merciless, Tarzan, Sheena, Clyde Beatty, and anybody played by Errol Flynn.

I was the most serious of the bunch. Small and agile, I would swing through my favorite maple tree and somersault into piles of rotting, sweet-smelling grass. "Apaches," I'd say, climbing onto the crossbeam of a picket fence and squinting across our Long Island lawn to an Arizona mesa, where thousands of Indians had silhouetted themselves against a technicolor sky—a sure sign of attack. Then, with a yell, I'd leap. To move in the air was to fly, to float in the endless space of my imagination, and I gave barely a thought to the earth that was rushing up to meet me. My world was full of grace and always would be.

SUMMER, years later. The sun smashes me into the baked earth of Moab, Utah. I stand in a crowd, squinting up at a man in a red cape and a sweatshirt that says "Captain Action," teetering thirty feet above me on the ledge of a converted Mormon church. His name is John Hagner, and he is sixty years old. Nearby, two of his friends hold a ribbon over two piled-up air mattresses, the kind that pole vaulters fall into. When John crashes through the ribbon, three days of festivities will end, and the Hollywood Stuntmen's Hall of Fame will be open for business.

Another friend, Lee Aakers—a part-time stuntman who once played the boy "Rusty" in "Rin Tin Tin"—aims at John with a shotgun. He fires, and we all jump. John clutches his chest and staggers along the ledge. He stiffens, sways for a moment like a freshly cut pine, and then, red cape swelling against the deep blue sky, tips forward into space.

AS A BOY in Baltimore, John Hagner sat for hours in the Saturday afternoon movies, studying the way lithe men and women fell off trains and leaped from castle walls in serials like "Spy Smasher," "Captain Marvel," and "Riders of the Whistling Skull." How could they do the superhuman without getting hurt? How the hero got the girl didn't matter—John wanted only to figure out the stunts and perform them for his friends. The way he saw it, the real drama came in riding a thousand-pound horse over a cliff into an icy river, and the real stars were the men and women who took over the reins to make the more famous actors look bigger than life.

When he was twelve, John went to the library and asked about stunts. "They pulled out a couple of books about *party tricks*," he says, still sounding shocked and hurt. "They had no idea what I was talking about." Soon he was corresponding with stuntmen in California and collecting behind-the-scenes photos, theater lobby cards, and other odds and ends. Later, he hung around movie sets until he got a job falling off a cliff for ten dollars a vertical foot. Eventually, he became a "fights and falls" man, a connoisseur of gravity called in to put on a bald skull cap, say, and dive down a flight of stairs for Telly Savalas. When he got to know stuntmen as co-workers, he was shocked again. "I used to think that most of them collected their own stuff. I found out that they didn't, and they were sorry."

That's why John founded the Hall of Fame, which now holds fifty thousand stills and negatives, a thousand videos of stunts and movies, and several tons of concrete slabs with footprints of the famous. (Famous inside the stunt world, that is. Although a few doubles like Errol Flynn and Burt Reynolds have leapt to the top of movie marquees, most of them whiz across the screen much too quickly to be recognized by anyone but their friends. That's another reason for the Hall.) John's prop collection is here, too: samurai swords that wouldn't hurt a rag doll, jackets rigged for flight, special shoes and hats and corsets, saddles with stirrups made to be jumped from. And somewhere in the basement, waiting for their own room, are at least five hundred penguins. John's been collecting them ever since 1948, when he was a sailor on an aircraft carrier supporting one of Admiral Byrd's expeditions to the South Pole. "Friends send them to me as Christmas presents," he says happily.

The founder and curator of all this retains the enthusiasm—and the body—of a twenty-year-old. Tall and lanky, John is handsome in an amiably craggy way. In his rawhide vest and cowboy hat, he looks like a retired gunslinger, the kind who looks up from a handful of cards to give advice to the new kid in town.

Moab itself might be likened to a cranky old prospector—Gabby Hayes, for instance—who goes it alone in a far corner of a state that's proud of its sober, clean-shaven image. A former uranium boom town, Moab lies in the heart of red-rock country, the burnt cliffs and slickrock desert, arches and twisted spires that have made the weirdly beautiful backdrop for dozens of westerns, including John Ford's "Cheyenne Autumn" and "The Searchers." North of town, the Colorado River curls out of a high-walled canyon, wanders muddily through a flood plain, then disappears between more sheer walls. Hundreds of curves and thousands of Indian petroglyphs later, those walls turn into the mile-high rims of the Grand Canyon. In summer, Moab fills with tourists and desert rats: rafters, hikers, mountain bikers—leathery ectomorphs who leave at dawn in jeeps and battered Road Warrior contraptions and return, sun-blasted and parched as prickly pear, in the early evening. During the day, the wide streets and motel swimming pools look emptier than the surrounding desert.

During cooler times of the year, I have explored some of this desert. But why am I here now?

"DON'T MOVE," says Richard Fraga, standing almost nose to nose with me and looking very intense, though odd, in a ten-gallon hat, t-shirt, cowboy boots, and shorts. "Movie-quality punches have to be whisker-close. Like this." He squares his shoulders and takes a couple of practice shots, lazy cross-overs that graze my beard. Suddenly, his fists disappear. I know they're out there whizzing by, though, because I feel a fluttering of hummingbird wings on both cheeks—a nice sensation in the 105-degree heat. When he finishes he says, "My students practice that all the time."

When he was small, Richard and his brothers spent days jumping in and out of moving cars and swinging from ropes tied to bridges. In high school, he raced motorcycles and dirt bikes and got hurt more badly than he has at any time since, though his ten-year stunt career has included a sixty-foot fall. Today—Thursday, the first day of the festival—he has driven in from California, where he runs Stunts West, a school for aspiring stunt artists.

"Stunts are much more controlled than competitive sports," he tells me. "I practice for days for something that takes just a couple of seconds in front of the camera. If I have to leap into a moving car through its window, I rehearse by diving again and again through a truck tire swinging from a rope. But stunts also require the mental capacity to adjust—sometimes in a split-second, and in mid-air—to different situations. You've got to make your body *talk*."

Talk? Judged by these high standards, my own body has been almost mute for years.

I look closely at Richard. He's about my age and size. There's even the hint of a gut. When he tells me about an agility test he gives to prospective students, I want badly to try it, but beat back the urge to ask.

Near us, in the mock western town that has sprung up next to the old Mormon church, John is getting ready to rehearse a fight with the group of Moab volunteers he's been training for several months. When they're ready to go, he walks over to some kids sitting on a low fence. "You guys can be the sound effects crew," he says, bending down. The kids get squirrelly with excitement. "When somebody gets hit on the chin, go BAM! and clap your hands. Okay? When they get it in the stomach, go OOF! Got that?" The kids nod vigorously.

John slaps dust from his vest and hands a tape recorder to Kim Renee, a young woman with long red hair who, like Richard, has just arrived. Her pick-up truck, still ticking from the long drive, says "STUNTWM" on its Nevada license plates. Kim once spent two television seasons jumping over trees and houses as a double for Wonder Woman, and she has already asked me if I'd like to see a photo of her seven-year-old son, Tony, in crash helmet and fireproof suit, jumping his motorcycle over a burning car. She picks up a bullhorn and puts it next to the speaker, turns on the recorder, and out comes a grainy version of "The Fistfight Fugue," or "The Chase

Concerto," or whatever you call that breathless, rousing music that always accompanies old-time frontier action.

A cowpoke in a black hat comes flying through the window of the "Rio Conchos Saloon," wobbles to his feet, and heads back in. Just then, a man bursts through the saloon's double doors, swings from an overhead beam, and drives both legs into Black Hat's stomach.

"OOF!" go the kids, leaping to their feet.

Black Hat rolls over backwards, gets up, and—"BAM!" shout the kids, almost on cue—slugs the other guy in the jaw. Down they crash, rolling in the dust. A tall sheriff tries to break things up. Down he goes, too, victim of a crunching right by John, who happens to be strolling by. Soon, six men and two women are punching and pulling hair and tossing each other into hay bales and over hitching rails. There's so much action that the kids, jumping up and down like pistons, start getting confused. "OOF!" they yell when somebody catches one on the chin, and John pauses in mid-punch and gasps, "No, it's 'BAM!' Remember?"

MOVIE MAYHEM is carefully orchestrated, every punch and fall plotted out. Over three days I watch John's group perform six times, and I see six identical fights. Another of the visiting pros, Jody McQueen, later tells me how he practices a single move. "Now let's take your crotch kicks," he says, backing up, all sinew and coiled reflex, like his famous brother Steve, whom he resembles. "What I do is drop a marble into an empty beer can, see, then hang the can by a string to exactly the height of my human target. Then I kick at it forty or fifty times in a row. If I hear a clank, I've kicked too far." He grins and cracks open a Budweiser, takes a sip. "Our main job as stuntmen is to make THE STAR look good. He gets all the glory and the money. We get no fame and only a little money. But we walk away from it standing tall."

Movie stuntman and director Hal Needham has said the key to not getting hurt is to stay "loose as warm spaghetti." But there's more to it than that. After John's saloon fight, I notice the forearm and elbow pads the brawlers wear under their long-sleeve shirts. Earlier, they'd softened the sun-hardened earth by hosing it down. Jody tells me that actors who intend to bounce off a wall study the wood first and aim for the soft spots between studs.

For a really dangerous "gag," like a fall from a galloping horse or a zooming car, a stunt double might dig a wide hole and fill it with dirt, ground cork and sawdust, then double-check the physics of the fall.

Sometimes, the stunt itself unfolds more slowly than it appears on film; three or more cameras that record the action at different speeds let technicians adjust the effects later in the editing room.

A feathery balsa wood chair slamming into your shoulder hurts a lot less than an oak one; an elbow pad tucked under a cowboy hat softens the blow of a "breakaway" beer bottle. Sugar candy makes a fine plate glass window to dive through, especially when sound effects are dubbed in later. About half of the pros at the festival tell me they've never been badly hurt. Still, accidents happen. One of the Hall's scarier photos shows a circle of assistants gripping a fire net and looking intently skyward while, five feet away, a man crashes shoulder-first into the grass. He looks just like Brueghel's Icarus plunging into the sea. (Miraculously, stuntman Harvey Parry wasn't badly hurt.)

For a Grade Z movie called "Hell's Angels '69," Jody McQueen was asked to skid his motorcycle under the trailer of a moving semi-truck. The idea was to scoot under, then kick the bike back up and keep going. Like his brother (who once lived in the warehouse that held his antique motorcycle collection), Jody had a reputation for making cars and bikes really talk. But this time he missed. The back wheels of the truck rolled over him, fracturing his skull and breaking his leg in 121 places. He lay in an eighty-six-pound body cast for three and a half years. Six years after the accident he was back at stunts. When I ask him why he still does it, he grins, puts his rawhide arms on his hips and says, "Well, now I'm finally learnin' *how*. Plus I'm stubborn as hell." The grin drifts off. Jody holds his hand inches from his face and says, "I seen the tread of that truck tire right *there*. And I can still see it."

I WAS a fifth grader, the reigning acrobat of the schoolyard, when the high chain-link fence in front of the swing set started to look very inviting. "Bet you can't jump it," said my friend Tommy, taking a running start on his swing, the chains jangling.

"Bet I could—if I wanted to." I leaned back and pumped hard, the way I had so often the year before, when Tommy and I had raced to be first to actually orbit the swing set. But as the wind began to roar in my ears and I pulled myself deeper and deeper into the sky, I glanced with each backswing at the row of stiff wire Xs that topped the fence. Somewhere in my mind I was calculating torque and acceleration and deceleration, and though I didn't know those words, I figured out soon enough that I couldn't make the jump. In fact, I knew I wasn't daring enough to try. I wasn't willing to say so, though, and on that day Tommy couldn't work up the courage to jump, either.

A few weeks later he did. I was home with the measles, so I didn't see it myself. But when I found out what had happened, I could imagine it—a wild-eyed boy flying in a great flailing arc until one of his ankles hooked the top of the fence.

By junior high, Tommy's limp had almost disappeared, and we'd drifted apart. Nobody said anything, but with my calculations and caution, I'd handed in my resignation to a dwindling fraternity, a league of the foolishly noble, the reckless and wild.

ONE OF THE FIRST things you see in the Hall of Fame is a wall-sized montage of paintings and photos depicting the early history of stunts in Hollywood. It hints at the profound changes in dramatic action wrought by film itself. "The greatest thing about picturemaking was the way it automatically did away with the physical limitations of the theater," Buster Keaton once said. "In the theater you had to create an illusion of being on a ship, a railroad train, or an airplane. The camera allowed you to show your audience the real thing."

In the montage, Keaton straddles the cow-catcher of a locomotive, cradling in his arms an absurdly large log. Nearby, Harry Houdini, hair smashed flat by the wind, hangs on to the wing struts of a tilting biplane. (Houdini's film career was brief, as was that of another genuine man of action who couldn't act, football star Red Grange.) Further along, Oliver Hardy thrashes neck-deep in a sidewalk mud-hole. Others ride horses over cliffs, tumble into waterfalls, and re-bound from the kind of exaggerated punches that only American heroes seem to get away with.

Early silent film stars were expected to do just about everything, and they used few doubles. "Perils of Pauline" star Pearl White did all her own stunts. So did Helen Gibson, a trick rider in wild west shows and the star of "The Hazards of Helen." In her most spectacular movie feat, Gibson crashed a motorcycle through a wooden gate, raced up a ramp, and jumped onto the flatcar of a speeding train.

Eventually, though, as actors became stars and audiences demanded more dangerous stunts, things changed. A star who had to rest a broken shoulder for several weeks could shut down an entire production. Better to hire rough and tumble substitutes like real cowboys who had better athletic skills and—more to the point—lower hourly rates and easier-to-replace faces. Professional high diver Bobby Dunn, working for Keystone Cops producer Mack Sennett, once dove eighty feet from a hotel roof into a water tank nine feet long, five feet wide, and five feet deep, a target that couldn't have looked any bigger than a postage stamp. He got five dollars. And that was after he'd lost an eye in an earlier, similar stunt.

Insurance companies had an effect, too. "They wouldn't insure a picture if I did the rough stuff," complained Errol Flynn. Still, Flynn held out longer than most for the chance to do the leaps, falls and swordfights he'd perfected in swashbucklers like "The Adventures of Robin Hood." Thus the rise of the stunt artist—the professional risk-taker.

Everyone I asked in Moab said that the greatest stuntman ever was Yakima Canutt. World Champion All-Round Cowboy from 1917 to 1923, Canutt coordinated the spectacularly dangerous chariot sequences in the 1959 "Ben Hur," but is best known as John Wayne's double in "Stagecoach." Falling beneath stampeding horses and clinging to the bottom of a careening stagecoach, he created stunts that couldn't be faked with clever camera angles, stunts that had never been imagined.

Canutt also made movie sets safer, inventing dozens of gadgets like the L-shaped "step stirrup" that lets a rider jump from a horse without catching a foot. He campaigned against the notorious Running W horse fall, an unconscionably cruel trip-wire technique that dropped an unsuspecting horse right in front of the camera, often killing or maiming it. "You can see Running Ws all over the place in old movies like 'The Charge of the Light Brigade,'" says John, who can spot one instantly in a finished film. Long outlawed in the U.S., it's still sometimes used in movies filmed partly in Mexico or other countries where it's legal. For all of this, Canutt received a special Oscar in 1967, the only one ever awarded to a stunt artist.

Almost everyone in Moab told stories about Canutt. "It's a little-known fact," one stuntman told me, "but Yak taught John Wayne his walk. Yup, he told the Duke he walked like a damn sissy."

ALL THROUGH the first day of the festival, the celebrities keep coming, a walking history of the stunt profession:

Bert Goodrich, the first Mr. America in 1939 and a double for Gene Autry, John Wayne, and others, who still looks boyish and bull-strong at eighty-one: "I never broke a bone, though once in a Buster Crabbe 'Tarzan' picture, I was swinging from a rope with a forty-pound dummy of Jane over my shoulder when the rope snapped. I hit a river bank and bounced about ten feet." He survived to do another take. Later on in real life, he opened up a string of health clubs and married Vic Tanny's sister.

Lee Diebold, who once jumped 225 feet from a helicopter into the ocean, a feat that sent him crashing into the water at about eighty miles per hour: "*Dee*bold's the name, *Die* Bold's the game," he tells me, shaking hands, then smiling shyly as I catch the pun.

Iron Eyes Cody, looking just like the Indian on an old nickel—a frieze of tragic nobility—whose career parallels the history of film itself, starting with his first job as an extra in 1919. He wanders around amiably signing autographs and taping everything on a home video camera for his grandchildren.

Wiry little Whitey Hughes, also a grandfather, who once coordinated four seasons' worth of human disaster for "Wild, Wild West," the "Citizen Kane" of the TV stunt business. Sixty-six years old, he just finished a movie in which he drove an eighteen-wheel rig at outrageous speeds down a curving mountain road. When I ask if he ever "practices" any of the high falls he's known for, he and his wife Dottie look at each other with disbelief, then practically fall down laughing.

AS THEY gather, the pros stand in clumps of two or three and tell stories, arms waving in shadowy punches. Many are meeting for the first time, though they seem to know each other's work. "Oh yeah, I saw that picture. Lotta good gags. Was that you who did the motorcycle transfer to the runaway truck? Slick work."

Richard Fraga asks John how he can help with an exhibition planned for the next afternoon in a downtown plaza. "If you want," Richard says, "I could jump out of a speeding car or something."

"Well, that would be nice," says John. "But you'll have to do it in an asphalt parking lot."

Richard shrugs. "Makes no difference to me."

I feel a tap on my arm. "Hey Mister, can I have your autograph?" A little boy is holding out a souvenir program that's been signed by Jody McQueen and a few others. I remember hearing Jody tell him: "Best of luck, kid. And whatever you do, don't get married until you're at least 35."

The boy presses a pen into my hand.

"But I'm not anybody famous," I say.

"Sign it anyway."

Maybe it's the boy. Maybe it's the sun, which is broiling my brains. But after a few minutes I take Richard aside and hear myself ask if, just for the sake of journalism, I can try the stuntman test he talked about. He smiles knowingly and nods. We stroll into the street—one of those vast avenues, wide as a river, that designate true western towns. "Okay." He folds his arms and takes the wide-legged stance of a football coach, all business. "Jog up to that parked car, turn around fast three times, and when you're halfway back jog in reverse for ten steps."

I touch my toes a couple of times, mainly for effect, and take off, suddenly hoping only to keep from tripping and banging the back of my head on the pavement. I surprise myself, though. My stride seems smooth, and all the way through—except for my first wobbly spin—I feel, in Richard's word, *controlled*. When I finish I close my eyes and grant myself a quick fantasy break: A huge sword comes swooshing at me. "HA!" I cry, leaping like Nureyev. The sword flashes under me and through a candelabra, wax flying everywhere. When I open my eyes, Richard is looking as intense as ever. "First of all, I gotta tell you that you run much better backwards than straight ahead."

MY FATHER and I had come to a sold-out Madison Square Garden so I could cheer for my hero, national high jump champ John Thomas, in his first duel with the unknown young Soviet who had taken away his world record. On his first jump, the rangy Thomas strode with long, slow steps, planted his take-off foot with a *Whump!*, and nonchalantly cleared the bar. There was scattered applause. Then the shorter, less-imposing looking Valery Brumel, who had been sitting in a chair with his arms folded and his back to the competition, walked to a tape mark on the floor. Just when I thought he would bend down to peel off his red sweats, he suddenly leaned forward, accelerated at an astonishing rate and sailed—not jumped— into the air with no sound at all. He floated over by about a foot. A kind of gasp came up around me, and I exchanged a look with my father. It was the most beautiful human movement I'd ever seen.

Almost every day during the next spring and summer, with visions of the deer-like Brumel in my head, I spent hours jumping over a bamboo pole in my backyard. A year later, in my first junior high competition, I took first in a large meet. It was my last win. Over the next few years, my competitors all turned into bean poles and learned to jump like frogs. But no matter how hard I worked for their lightness, the arc of my own brief flights seemed to get flatter and flatter.

ON FRIDAY afternoon, Richard Fraga and Jody McQueen get hold of a nicely maintained pale yellow Ford LTD that belongs to Moab Mayor Tom Stocks, who can't possibly realize what they are about to do to it. First they take out all the loose items in the car, glove compartment, and trunk. They unscrew the antenna, wire down the battery, pry off the hubcaps, pump the rear tires up to sixty pounds and soften the front ones, adjust one of the brakes to help the car skid on target, and secure the trunk, hood, and all the windows with wide silver slashes of duct tape.

We are at the downtown plaza. After several screeching practice runs with Jody driving, Richard adjusts his hip and elbow pads and bends down to brush some pebbles from his proposed landing strip on the asphalt. Despite the heat, a crowd has gathered. Instamatics appear and parents hoist children to their shoulders.

Having studied the asphalt like a map, Richard strides to the far end of the lot where Jody sits in the roughly idling car, the driver's door wide open and the air conditioner blasting. John's local stunt team comes on and performs its usual good-natured brawl.

The applause trickles off, and the taped-up LTD comes flying. Jody jams on the brakes, sending the car into a screaming smoking sideways skid. The passenger door opens and out flies Richard, headfirst. He hits the asphalt hard—no fudging this one with speeded-up cameras—and rolls a few times. Jody jumps out of the car, grabs Richard, and slams him against the passenger door. Richard sends Jody across the hood with a flurry of punches. Jody quivers, crumples to the ground and lies still. "OK, I'm dead," he says. The crowd cheers. "Wow!" says a little boy standing near me.

Jody got into stunts because he wanted attention. "Steve and I liked show business because we came from the broken family type thing," he says, examining a red gouge in his arm, a souvenir from his fight with Richard. "We were raised by our aunt and uncle, but they had their own kids to look after, so we felt like outlaws, and we just did anything to get looked at, run away and what all—you notice how Steve's best movies are all escapes? Then when television came out back in the hills"—in Slater, Missouri—"every Saturday night everyone gathered around it and they ignored me, I didn't care what I did, fall off a chair or jump from the refrigerator. I asked my school teacher—I was ten years old before I went to school—I asked her what that was in the TV, and she said 'Hollywood.' I said, 'You mean, those are real people doin that?' And I got to thinkin, that's where I wanna be. If they're gettin the attention, I want in there."

Jody then said something that I eventually heard, in one form or another, from practically everyone. "When I got to Hollywood, I somehow already knew how to do the stunts. Nobody had to teach me. It was like I came from a different time or something. I can't really explain it. All I know is that stunt talent's just a natural thing, and it's rare as chicken lips."

ON SATURDAY, there's a big parade. Leading it is Monty Montana, the trick roping rodeo star, who the festival program says, "has roped more Presidents at various functions than any other cowboy." As he prances down Main Street on his horse Rex, the sun bounces off his white ten-gallon hat and the blue eagle on his red shirt. Like so many of the old-timers, he looks terrific.

When the parade breaks up at the Hall of Fame, Monty sits on Rex and gently lassos surprised tourists, thanking them for not breaking his rope as they wriggle free. Inside the Hall, the Induction Ceremony begins. After showing Bert Goodrich how to work his video camera, Iron Eyes Cody comes to the dais and gives an Indian prayer in hand signs. John Hagner warms up the crowd by telling hammy jokes, then balances an amazing variety of objects on his chin—a sword, deer antlers, a four-foot fish, a ukulele. Bert Goodrich takes the ukulele, announces that Mae West once encouraged him in his singing, and in a high, reedy voice that seems incongruous with his muscles, sings a ballad about his life, calling stuntmen "actors in the sky."

Actors in the sky. I like that. As Bert bangs on at the ukulele, his thick white hair bouncing on his forehead, I begin to drift, that phrase ringing over and over. I dream that the air is filling with stuntmen, those brave and wonderful athletes who lend their reality to our illusions, soaring and falling through the brilliant desert sky. And I imagine among them a boy straining against gravity, trying to find the right gesture, the perfect words, the first few steps of the dance that will allow an awkward, ordinary life to break into beauty.

Finally, we all go outside for the ribbon-breaking. John Hagner puts on his red cape and climbs a long ladder to the roof. Two friends pull the ribbon across the mats. Others set themselves as spotters. Richard Fraga calls out for quiet.

I watch intently. A shotgun blast. John clutches his chest, sways, and slowly tips forward, his cape fanning out like wings. By squinting and concentrating hard, I can just about stop him in mid-fall. I can make him fly, fly through the endless space of my imagination. He moves with the grace that I and the others around me have wished for in movies and in dreams—dying, but reprieved for an instant from our mortal limits.

Postscript

That's it. "Actors in the Sky" is serious, ambitious—and far different from anything I could have imagined way back at the Moab restaurant where I first noticed the "Grand Opening" flyer.

How do I like it? Well enough, I think. It still gives off energy when I read it, and it's as true as I can make it to what I experienced in Moab and within myself—what many of us experience, no matter what our backgrounds, when we bump up against our "mortal limits." I'm satisfied with the portraits of the main characters and the dramatic movement in most of the scenes.

As for my role in the story: sometimes I worry that I intrude or that the personal flashbacks don't quite mesh; sometimes I feel just fine up there on center stage. I'm still too close to the writing to know for sure. Sentences are still bouncing around inside my skull.

And I'm bothered by much of what I left out. As I said earlier, I believe what's cut from a story is as important as what's put in, and sometimes, like a sculptor chipping away at stone, a writer writes by process of elimination. Although I wrote "final" versions of more than forty pages of scenes and character sketches, I felt that my narrative drive just couldn't support much more . . . stuff.

Here for instance is a page of almost-final draft that I cut in half:


```
picture if I did the rough stuff," complained Errol Flynn, who held out longer
Nevertheless, Flynn held out longer than probably any other actor
for the chance to keep doing the kind of leaps, falls and sword-
fights he'd perfected in spectacles like "The Adventures of Robin
Hood" (my idea of the greatest movie ever, until I saw "Gunga
Din"). Thus the rise of the hired specialist--the movie
stuntman.
        One of the earliest stunt experts was Yakima Canutt, who had
```

~~been~~ World Champion All Round Cowboy, ~~from 1917 to 1923.~~ Canutt, ~~who~~ coordinated the [spectacular] chariot sequences in the 1959 "Ben Hur," [but his] ~~is~~ most admired by the pros for his daring inventions doubling for John Wayne in "Stagecoach." [twenty years earlier.] Falling beneath a team of stampeding horses or clinging to the bottom of a careening stagecoach, he created stunts that ~~were impossible to~~ [couldn't be faked] fake with clever camera angles, stunts ~~that had never been done before.~~ /It's no surprise that he did some of his most spectacular work in John Ford movies. Ford loved working with stuntmen and started his own career as one; he broke an arm escaping from an exploding automobile and once ruined a carefully staged scene by blessing himself before leaping from a train into a river far below. [ouch!]

Canutt also contributed to safety on the set, [made movie sets safer by] inventing ~~dozens of~~ devices like the L-shaped "step stirrup" that allowed a rider to jump from a horse without catching a foot. He campaigned against ~~cruel and~~ [And cruel & unusual treatment] unconscionably dangerous ways ~~of~~ treating animals, ~~The most notorious was~~ [like] the Running 'W' horse fall, where unsuspecting horses were tripped by wires and often killed or maimed. "You can see Running Ws all over the place in

Out went passages I felt only half-hearted interest in. For instance, the little I wrote about former child star Lee Aakers was easy to cut; he didn't play a major role in Moab and didn't pique my interest enough for me to really ask him what he'd been doing all these years.

Much more painfully, though, out went wonderful stories from Kim Renee and Bert Goodrich and, especially, Whitey Hughes. Out went entire characters such as Kenny Hill, who's not a professional "fights and falls" man at all, but a mild-mannered New Jersey policeman who spends his vacations hanging around western movie sets with his heroes, the stuntmen. It hurt to see these folks go, especially when they spent so much time answering my questions.

And out from the story went someone else who was there: SueEllen

Campbell, who is now my wife and who drove with me to Moab and mingled with the guests, too. She has appeared in several of my stories, especially in travel pieces that describe things we've actually done together. But here, because she didn't have much to do with my fascination with stunt artists, I quite unguiltily deleted her.

She also happens to be a teacher, a writer, and my sharpest—my most unsparing and fair—editor. I'm a pretty good proofreader (thanks to lots of reading and some demanding elementary school teachers, my skills with the basic writing tools of spelling, grammar and punctuation have always been strong). But SueEllen is better. Much more important, she responds to my work as an articulate reader who demands a good *story*, no matter what the subject. And because she knows me so well, she can tell me if I'm writing near the top of my form—or well below it.

Do good friends and relatives make good readers of your work? Not usually. Then how do you find a good critic? Like most writers do: through trial and error. I'm very lucky to have found such a good one so close to home.

And now it's Show Time: time to mail this story out.

Chapter 6

Getting It Out . . .
Getting It Back

How to Prepare a Manuscript and What to Do When It Comes Back

AT LAST, I'M ready to mail my story—probably the most exciting single step in the writing process.

But this means more than just stuffing the pages into a manila envelope and slapping on a few stamps. First I've got to prepare the manuscript, pick out a place to send it to, and write a cover letter that will help—not hurt—its chances for success.

Manuscript Preparation

The nuts and bolts of proofreading and manuscript preparation are clearly explained in many good books, including the freelance writer's bible, *Writer's Market* (described in detail in chapter seven), so let me point out just a few things.

Produce a clean manuscript. Long before an editor gets to your knockout final paragraph, or even to those great quotes on page two, he or she has formed some strong opinions about you based on your first several sentences and—far more than you might imagine—on the condition of your manuscript. If the pages look sloppy—marred by fingerprints or smudged erasures, the telltale paper clip imprint from a previous submission, odd margins, fuzzy typeface from worn typewriter or printer ribbons, spelling mistakes, penciled-in last-minute changes—the editor will assume, with probable good cause, that your writing and your thinking are sloppy, too.

Don't give the editor that chance. By the time you've finished writing a story, you're probably too close to it to pick out the inevitable typos, so try one or both of these proofreading tricks. Read your manuscript backwards, a sentence at a time. This will keep you from getting caught up in the flow of the narrative, the lyricism of the language, and you may actually catch a few of the careless errors you'd have glided past otherwise. Or, give your manuscript to a trusted friend whose knowledge of spelling and grammar is better than yours.

This doesn't mean that your ten-page story will come winging back through the mails because of a single comma error or your last-minute, neatly penciled-in correction on page seven. You can also waste time and energy by fanatically retyping or reformatting an adequate layout. One of my pet peeves is the perfectly typed manuscript, suitable for framing in the Louvre, that has nothing interesting to say. This sort of rage for order reminds me of a sign I used to pass every day on the door of one of my CSU colleagues: Beautiful writing cannot save banal ideas.

Be professional. Avoid looking like an amateur. Do NOT write "Copyright 1989" or "First North American Serial Rights Only" or any other foolishness on a cover page (which you don't need for anything shorter than a book) or on page one. These legal considerations are either assumed or, more likely, clearly stated in the guidelines of the publication to which you're submitting. You're expected to be familiar with them. (See chapter seven for more on writer's rights.)

Always SASE. SASE or SAE means a self-addressed stamped envelope big enough for your manuscript. A story should never leave home without it. A cynic might say that it lets editors reject your masterpiece that much faster. A realist knows that no publication can afford the time and money to return hundreds or thousands of manuscripts a year.

The Cover Letter

Not long ago I heard the editor of a prominent literary magazine say that she *automatically* returns any manuscript not accompanied by a cover letter. It's just plain rude to leave one out, she explained; it's like somebody marching up to you, saying "Read this," and then walking away.

Not all editors may feel so vehement, but I think a cover letter is a common decency that the editor, as simply another human being, deserves. It also lets the person who rips open your envelope know that *you're* human, too. Here's the one I put in the mail with "Actors in the Sky."

Department of English
Colorado State University
Fort Collins, CO 80523
(303) 491-6428

Charles McGrath
Assistant Managing Editor
The New Yorker
25 W. 43rd St.
New York, NY 10036

Dear Mr. McGrath,

Would you please consider for publication my enclosed new essay, "Actors in the Sky," which is about Hollywood stunt artists. I researched this story in Moab, Utah, where I recently attended a three-day grand-opening festival for the Hollywood Stuntmen's Hall of Fame. I hope you enjoy the story.

I have published other nonfiction in *Audubon, Ohio, The Runner, Miami Herald Tropic* and elsewhere; and fiction in *North American Review, Carolina Quarterly* and other journals. I'm an assistant professor of English at Colorado State University, where I teach fiction and nonfiction writing workshops in the MFA creative writing program.

I'm hoping to hear from you soon.

Sincerely,

John Calderazzo

Yes, *The New Yorker*. I've certainly worked hard enough, so I might as well shoot for the top of the line, even if the numbers are overwhelmingly against me and the tone doesn't strike me as *quite* right for that fascinating magazine. Next on my list are *Harper's* and *Atlantic*. How about something that specializes in the entertainment industry, like *TV Guide?* No way. The story's much too long, too "interior," too literary. It's simply the wrong product for that market.

Notice how the letter gets right to the point without, I hope, sounding blunt. I try not to waste time with idle chatter ("You should have been there, too. The sun shone spectacularly on . . ."). I avoid buttering up the editor with obviously phony sentiments like, "I've really loved your magazine down through the years." Finally, I offer a quick, clean summary of my publication history, not a three-page resume or testimonials to my brilliance ("My creative writing teacher says this is the best thing she's read in years!"). Editors want to decide those things for themselves.

What if you've published nothing at all? It's true that well-published writers often do get read more carefully by editors (that's why I always put in my little brag-list), but it's also true that first-time authors are published in national magazines probably every day of the year. An excellent opening paragraph to a compelling, well-researched story will make a reader quickly forget your amateur status.

Okay, you've cleaned up the manuscript, addressed and stamped the return envelope, and written the cover letter. Finally, finally, finally, it's time to send that story out!

Replies from Editors: "Sorry," "Maybe," "Yes!"

Off goes your story into the mails. What's next? Many possibilities.

You hear nothing. Very unlikely, but manuscripts do get lost. Imagine that your office or bedroom is a magazine office. Every day the mail brings ten to twenty manila folders. That's maybe 100 a week, more than 5000 a year—not unusual for a national publication. Could you keep track of them all, keep them from the jaws of your hungry dog, remember when they slide behind the bureau? *Writer's Market* lists the reply time of magazines. Add 50 percent to it. If you hear nothing by then, send a postcard politely reminding the editor of your submission. If in a few weeks you still hear nothing, assume that the editor has been whisked to Mars and send your story somewhere else.

You get rejected. Welcome to the club. Not long ago, at the end of the first class meeting of my senior-level fiction writing workshop at CSU,

I walked up and down the aisles and slapped a small rectangle of paper on every student's desk:

> Thank you for your submission,
> but the editors feel that your
> work is not right for our
> publication.

"Okay," I said, "now you've all been rejected. Indiscriminately. And you never even showed me your work! You might as well get used to it. Now go home and write your best stuff and don't worry what anybody else says about it."

Rejection is inevitable. When you get that first deadly little slip, unadorned with handwriting or any other signs of human life, you can respond by calling the editor an idiot or throwing out or furiously rewriting your story. You think that you'll never be a writer, that the editor may well be an idiot (dolts are always getting elected to public office, so why shouldn't they occasionally show up on a magazine masthead?), but your one rejection doesn't prove anything. You may have sent your piece to the wrong publication; the editor may simply have different tastes from yours; he or she may not have even read it—a first reader may have rejected it. It may have made the top ten of the four hundred stories received during the month, but the magazine had room for only two. Still, you could have made the 97th or 98th percentile.

Hang tough. Have a little faith in yourself. Send it out again. And again. After a while, of course, you have to wonder if all those editors out there aren't really on to something: your story needs work. Only you can be the judge of that. But not after just one or two rejections.

Sometimes the rejection form will come back with some actual handwriting: "Sorry" or "The final vote went against it." Although always heartbreaking and frequently illegible, these are clear invitations to send another story soon—not any old junk you've got lying around, but something at least as good as your original submission.

Much more rarely, an editor will request to see a rewritten version of your story. This is NOT a promise of publication, so you may have a tough decision here. You may strongly disagree with the editor's suggestions, in which case you should at least acknowledge the interest with a note. You may make some or all of the requested changes and still see the story rejected. Or you may do the work and—at last, at last—get published. In weighing your decision, you can often gauge the interest of the editor by the quality of his or her suggestions. A casual "Tighten it all around and show it to us again" might not be worth your time. But a page of single-spaced comments may reveal sensitivity and enthusiasm you'd be wise to follow up on. As Humphrey Bogart says at the end of "Casablanca," this might be the beginning of a beautiful friendship.

Or maybe some wise, wise editor will accept your work immediately. Beware. The story may not appear in quite the same form as you wrote it. Good editors, if they have time, will send you galleys (the first typeset version of your story) with editorial changes, or at least ask your permission to make changes. Others may make a few small adjustments without telling you anything, or, if they're especially rude or self-important, they may fiddle like mad with your meticulously crafted sentences—sometimes improving them, sometimes not.

And sometimes—wonder of wonders—your story will break into print *exactly* as you wrote it.

Chapter 7

Getting It Done *Again*
Resubmit · Resell · Rejoice

WHY RECYCLE ONLY aluminum cans and newspapers? Why not words?

Like the words in your last story, the one that took you two weekends to research and every evening for a week to write. The one your local newspaper paid you $20 for, about what a kid bagging groceries makes on a slow night. Think about it: throwing away newsprint that can be used again obviously wastes valuable resources. Why abandon a valuable story after just one publication?

Whether you want to live entirely by your writing or just hang onto your self-respect by making a few pennies above minimum wage, you've got to know something about reworking and/or reselling stories. If you think this commercialism is beneath you, consider the fact that fiction writers do it all the time. A "short story" that's published in *The New Yorker* or *Redbook* often shows up months or years later "in somewhat different form" (as the small print on the copyright page often puts it) as a chapter in a novel. If the writer is lucky, it may surface again in an annual collection like *Best American Stories* or a college reader like *The Norton Anthology of Contemporary Short Fiction*. Better yet, Hollywood might want to buy an option on the book (that is, purchase the exclusive right to just *consider* making a movie out of it). A paycheck sweetens each of these already sweet occasions, and I don't hear too many fiction writers saying, "Oh no, don't pay me *again!*"

The stunt artist story you've been watching me research and write took several weeks and several hundred dollars of my savings, not counting the time lost to other money-making ventures. I've yet to get back a penny. Sooner or later, I think, a magazine or literary journal will take it. But unless I publish it a second time or at least write some "slant stories," I might as well bag groceries. (Of course, using it as the subject matter for this book isn't a bad example of recycling.)

And now I think it is time to stop talking about stunt artists. I'm *sick* of them by now, and you must be, too.

Let's talk instead about . . . boomerangs. Boomerangs, of all things, taught me how to write to different kinds of audiences and, eventually, make a full-time living by writing.

I encountered my first flying stick several years ago, while I was sitting one day at the kitchen table of my home in northwest Ohio. Outside, for the second straight week, the sky was camouflaging itself as soiled laundry, and my spirits weren't much brighter. As I idly leafed through a mail order catalogue that was lying on the table, I brooded about the fact that I just wasn't making it as a freelance writer, even though practially everything I wrote was getting published. Then, on a page of the catalogue devoted to sports clothes, a photograph caught my eye.

A very athletic-looking guy was leaping into the air to catch a boomerang. Interesting, I thought. When I was a kid I'd often wondered how they worked—if they worked. Now I looked closer at the picture. Beneath the athletic-looking guy, who I'd assumed was a model, were some tiny words:

Chet Snouffer, Delaware, Ohio
National Boomerang Champion

Whrrrrr . . . On came the flywheel of curiosity. Boomerang throwers had competitions? Did the most crooked thrower win?

How could I find out *and* maybe make some money to pay the rent? Well, *Ohio Magazine* had recently bought some of my profiles, such as the Grand Rapids flood story, and since my map indicated that Delaware was only a couple of hours south . . . That night I traced Chet Snouffer through directory assistance and gave him a call.

To jump ahead: Chet sounded fun, knew more about boomerangs

than I thought there was to know, and sent me a boomerang news-letter that he mimeographed at home and mailed all over the world. "The Leading Edge" opened my eyes to a universe of boomerang esoterica, including the fact that an American team led by Chet had beaten the Australians at their own game, and that PhD dissertations had been written about the aerodynamics of the things. A few weeks later, when the sky finally cleared, I drove down to Delaware, met Chet in the middle of a giant empty field, and spent the afternoon talking and throwing "booms."

I was confident enough about the freshness of this material and my good relations with *Ohio* to just plunge in and write a profile of Chet without querying the magazine. Why a personal profile? Because I liked the form, and the bulk of my information suited it well.

Here's the way (after the usual false starts) I opened that story. Read it carefully so you can compare it with what I wrote later when I tried to resell it.

ZEN AND THE ART OF BOOMERANG THROWING
The Many Happy Returns of Chet Snouffer

Chet Snouffer stands in a grassy field in Delaware, Ohio, and prepares to practice his fifteen-thousand-year-old art. He ceremoniously tosses some grass into the air, then turns at a right angle to the breeze. He picks up a delicate-looking, delta-shaped stick, reaches back and throws. With a soft *whir* the stick flies end over end for about forty yards, and then curves left, steadily left, simultaneously flattening itself out and beginning to glide. It swoops up above the treeline, flashes in the sun and rides the breeze back in. It slows to an almost stationary hover over Chet's outstretched hands and drops gently down.

The boomerang has flown beautifully—in all, farther than the length of a football field—and Chet has walked a total of five steps to meet it. It's not good enough, though. The National Championships, in Fairfax, Virginia, are only three days away, and if Chet wants to keep his reputation as one of the most skilled boomerang throwers in the world, he must do better.

"Wind's a little stiff today," he says, an easy smile brightening . . .

You get the idea. Even though most of the sentences describe the flight of the boomerang, which I felt was crucial to an understanding of the story, the title and the opening line clearly fix the focus on Chet. Furthermore, the profile portrays a human being in *action,* a narrative trick which always helps engage a reader. (Interviewing people while they are *doing* things usually helps me get this sort of information.) The present tense conveys further dramatic tension.

I write carefully and slowly. This meticulousness helps explain the high rate of acceptance I was enjoying even as a nonfiction beginner—and my low bank account. Counting travel time, library research ("fifteen-thousand-year-old art"), writing, and final, pre-computer-days typing, I spent at least ten days on the 3000-word story. Not long after I mailed it, *Ohio* called to say they'd like to print it, and how about $450?

That may sound like pretty good money. But think of it this way: pro-rated at $45 per full workday, it came to about $11,000 a year before taxes, provided I sold everything I wrote and didn't stall in mid-story or take any of the "down time" I often need between projects.

So what did I say to *Ohio*'s offer? "Great!" With a few minor word changes and a new title—the more effective "SWOOSH" (editors never seem to like my titles)—this version of the story became Publication Number One.

During this time, I'd been attending meetings of a Toledo-area writer's group with the very uncatchy name of Northwest Ohio Writer's Forum. Like a lot of such groups, it didn't teach me much about writing itself (I didn't expect it to), but it did put me in touch with fellow strugglers—a community of sympathizers—plus the occasional local media celebrity who came to speak. One of these pros was Norm Richards, who turned out to be far from "local." Norm had been editor of *Chicago Magazine,* the model for so many of today's city magazines, and was now editor of *Marathon World,* the handsome, well-heeled publication of the Marathon Oil Company, whose world headquarters happened to be in nearby Findlay.

Like the publications of many large corporations, *Marathon World* was sent to all employees and stockholders of the company—a wide variety of people—and therefore contained not just the staff-written oil business articles I'd expected, but at least two general interest features in every issue. These were often written by freelancers. In keeping with its Ohio base, Norm told our group, the magazine leaned toward midwestern subjects.

Like boomerang throwers? I wondered a few days later, as I paged carefully through the *Marathon World*s at the public library. Unless you've somehow produced one of those rare pieces of writing that transcends the partisan nature of most publications, it's crucial to send your work to a market that's appropriate for it. Perfectly good stories mailed to the "wrong" places trigger at least as many rejection slips as lifeless or shoddy writing.

But how does a beginner learn the market?

Well, as just about every editor on earth says, "The best way to find out what kind of writing we're looking for is to read our publication." In other words, put aside a few hours, go to the nearest library periodicals section, and start turning pages.

The next best method—and by far the quickest way to start—is to consult *Writer's Market,* the two-inch-thick freelance writer's bible that lists thousands of places to sell your "articles, books, fillers, gags, greeting cards, novels, plays, scripts, and short stories!" Here's a typical entry:

WORKING WOMAN, Hal Publications, Inc., 342 Madison Ave., New York NY 10173. (212)309-9800. Executive Editor: Julia Kagan. Editor: Anne Mollegen Smith. 85% freelance written. Works with a small number of new/unpublished writers each year. Monthly magazine for executive, professional and entrepreneurial women. "Readers are ambitious, educated, affluent managers, executives, and business owners. Median age is 34. Material should be sophisticated, witty, not entry-level, and focus on work-related issues." Circ. 900,000. Pays on acceptance. Publishes ms an average of 8 months after acceptance. Byline given. Offers 20% kill fee after attempt at rewrite to make ms acceptable. Buys all rights, first rights for books, and second serial (reprint) rights. Submit seasonal/holiday material 6 months in advance. Computer printout submissions acceptable only if legible; prefers letter-quality. Sample copy for $2.50 and 8½x12 SAE; writer's guidelines for SAE with 1 first class stamp.
Nonfiction: Julia Kagan, executive editor. Jacqueline Johnson, book excerpts editor. Book excerpts; how-to (management skills, small business); humor; interview/profile (high level executive or entrepreneur preferred); new product (office products, computer/high tech); opinion (issues of interest to managerial, professional, entrepreneur women); personal experience; technical (in management or small business field); and other (business). No child-related pieces that don't involve work issues; no entry-level topics; no fiction/poetry. Buys roughly 200 mss/year. Query with clips of published work. Length: 250-3,000 words. Pays $50-750. Pays the expenses of writers on assignment.
Photos: State availability of photos with ms.
Columns: Management/Enterprise, Basia Hellwig; Manager's Shoptalk, Louise Washer; Lifestyle, Food, Freddi Greenberg; Fitness, Health, Janette Scandura; Business Watch, Michele Morris; Computers, Technology, Anne Russell. Query with clips of published work. Length: 1,200-1,500 words. Pays $400.
Tips: "Be sure to include clips with queries and to make the queries detailed (including writer's expertise in the area, if any). The writer has a better chance of breaking in at our publication with short articles and fillers as we prefer to start new writers out small unless they're very experienced elsewhere. Columns are more open than features. We do not accept phone submissions."

To translate:

• The first good news I see here is "85% freelance written." This means that staff members and agented writers aren't likely to crowd you out, although you'll probably be competing with hordes of freelancers.

• Editor Smith describes the magazine's readers to help you, the writer, aim your story at a well-defined audience—one that's long been a part of the professional workforce. If your query letter or manuscript assumes otherwise—"Are you tired of lugging laundry up the stairs while other women climb the corporate ladder?"—your story will go down the drain.

- "Pays on acceptance" is more happy news; you'll get your money as soon as the magazine says yes. Less good news would be "Pays on publication," which could easily occur a year or more after acceptance. The bigger the publication, the farther ahead it plans.

- "Kill fee" is the amount you are promised for an officially assigned story even if, for any number of unanticipated reasons (the health nut you profiled dropped dead, a new editor doesn't like your style), the magazine rejects your finished product. It's usually 20 to 33 percent of the original fee.

- "Buys all rights" is a warning that the periodical owns your story forever; you won't be able to resell the piece to another magazine—unless the first magazine gives you permission (which is often the case). "Buys first rights only" are the words you *really* want to see.

- "Writer's Guidelines" are simply more detailed versions of the *Writer's Market* entries. They're helpful, but, again, no substitute for studying the publication itself.

Writer's Market has all this, plus a list of agents, a glossary of terms ("Cutline," "Desk-top publishing"), tips on manuscript preparation, a quick guide to writer's rights, and more. Updated yearly, it's easy to find in bookstores and libraries. (See Good Books at the end of the book for other guides to the market.)

Okay, now that you've picked out a home for your writing, your next task is to soften up the home-owner—the editor. There are two ways to do this.

One, launch your completed story cold and shivering into the mail, like Moses on the Nile, and hope that your exhaustive research, brilliant ideas, and compelling voice catch an editor on a very, very good day. That worked for the first stories I wrote for *Audubon* (about the maker of the Swiss Army knife) and *Ohio,* but I had slaved over those manuscripts and didn't know yet how badly the odds were stacked against me.

Two, write a query letter. This is the approach I finally took with *Marathon World,* which I concluded would make a nice home indeed for a second boomerang story. Here's what I sent:

Dear Mr. Richards,
    What do you call a boomerang that doesn't come back? A stick. But boomerangs *do* come back, as more and more people—from weekend throwers to hard-core competitors—are discovering to their delight. In fact, recent years have seen a boom in American boomeranging, a zany sport that has included:

—A Smithsonian Institution "Throw-In" on the National Mall in Washington, D.C., that drew thousands of people and offered trophies like the Douglas MacArthur "I Shall Return" Cup.

—An American team led by Chet Snouffer, of Delaware, Ohio, that recently beat the Australians at their own, 15,000-year-old-game.

—Demonstrations of the infamous "William Tell in Reverse," a trick in which a thrower pins an apple to the top of his cap, fires his boomerang, then positions himself under its return flight so that— *thwack!*—it cracks the apple in two.

I think that your readers would be very interested in a 2,000-word feature story about these articulate athletes and their fascination with this little-understood flying stick. I've been talking with several nationally-ranked throwers and can provide ample quotations about what enthusiasts call "The thinking man's frisbee."

I'm a freelance writer who has published articles and essays in *Audubon, Ohio, The Runner* and other magazines.

Enclosed are a few clips. I'm hoping to hear from you soon.

> Sincerely,
> John Calderazzo

"Most writers have trouble with queries," says Tom Morrisey, who has read thousands. A veteran writer, magazine editor and Director of Publications for the Quarton Group of Troy, Michigan, he explains:

> In writing a query, the writer is thrust into the role of *salesman*— someone who thinks quickly on his feet, likes to meet people and prefers conversation to reflection. Writers—the good ones—lean the other way on virtually all counts.
>
> That's the only way I can explain some of the query letters I receive, which sound like written versions of late-night used-car commercials. The writer is so uncomfortable with the task at hand that he produces a hyped-up parody. It's painful to write, painful to read. It's far easier to 'sell' your story with a friendly, uncontrived letter that tells the editor two things: Why the story is right—at this time—for this magazine. Why you're the right person to do the story.[11]

In light of Tom's comments, my long-ago query letter, one of my first, doesn't look too awful. Yes, it leans toward "hype"—and I would tone it down if I were writing it today—but I think a genuine sense of enthusiasm for the topic overcomes that. Used-car salesmen need not worry about competition from me. The letter could do a better job of angling the story to *Marathon.* Chet was my only midwestern connection, although at least I made it obvious he was from Ohio, and I did mention my projected length, which I based on my examination of the magazine. It does a decent job of tantalizing the editor by *not* telling the whole story; if it did, what would the editor have to look forward to? I think I made a good case for my qualifications. The letter's packed with information, hinting, therefore, at much more to come. Among my clips was my first boomerang story from *Ohio*.

But what if I'd had no good-looking clips or any publications at all? How would an editor have known I could write? Well, there's the letter itself—a one-page sample of writing and organizing ability. That's why I started *instantly* with a hook, a boomerang joke I'd heard only a few days earlier, and tried to keep it lively throughout. In case you're wondering, the abrupt start is a common practice among freelancers; editors expect it—they learn fast whether you've got the right story for them. You also learn whether that story is for you; if you can't compress the main ideas and highlights into a page or so, you may not understand or care about the topic enough to write about it yet.

As a teacher, I'd give my letter a B + and send it back for fine-tuning. At the time, though, it was the best I could do, and so off it went to *Marathon World*.

Back came the reply: Yes! An official assignment confirmed with a contract that specified subject, length, due date (uncomfortably soon), fee ($1000—worth the discomfort) and expense allowances. In an attached note, Norm mentioned how he'd chuckled over my opening joke, which set him up for the rest of my pitch. Then he reminded me about the magazine's midwestern constituency and suggested I discuss other boomerang throwers from Indiana, Kansas, Illinois.

But I didn't know any. Except for Chet, the only ones I'd heard of lived on the East Coast or in Australia. Soon I was back in contact with Chet, getting names and addresses of midwestern subscribers to his newsletter. I drafted a form letter describing my assignment and sent it with an SASE to a dozen strangers: ". . . you might tell me how you got interested in boomerang throwing; what it means to your life (solemnity not allowed!); something offbeat or humorous . . ." At least half of them responded within a week, thank God. I took the best of their comments and incorporated them into a story heavy with details from the *Ohio* story.

THE BOOMERANG
That Magnificent Flying Machine

Consider the boomerang, that magnificent flying machine. A slim crooked stick sanded and polished to a shiny finish, it is all wing. Thrown overhand like a peg to second base, it flies end over end toward a distant line of trees, then curves, flattens out, spins, swoops, and all the while traces a serene and bird-like arc through the air. Riding the breeze back home, it slows, hovers for a moment above an outstretched hand, and drops gently down. Beautiful. Baseball, helicopter, glider, hawk, feather, the boomerang seems at once the most complicated and simplest of miracles—a flight of fancy come to life.

No wonder this floating piece of wood has captured the imagination of so many. The last few years have seen a boom in American boomeranging, especially in the Midwest. What else could explain the curious request of Edna Gottemoeller, of Sydney, Ohio? A year ago, when she was planning a family reunion for her three daughters, three sons, and twelve grandchildren, Mrs. Gottemoeller decided to add a boomerang throw to the festivities. "Please advise me," she wrote to Smithsonian Institution archivist and boomerang expert Ben Ruhe. "What is the best model boomerang for a lady of 70 weighing 100 pounds who is a fast runner? I intend to make a good showing at the fling."

Note the difference from the first story. The title and the first and last sentences of the opening paragraph shift the focus from a person to the boomerang as phenomenon, yet I've been able to salvage much of my earlier description of the boomerang in flight—a big savings of time (in fact, the story took about a quarter of the time of the first one). The second paragraph guides the story into *Marathon*'s midwestern groove; and Mrs. Gottemoeller, the "lady of 70 weighing 100 pounds who is a fast runner," quickly provides humor and offbeat human interest after the impersonal, somewhat reverent opening paragraph.

Publication Number Two. Total earnings: $1450, plus a very slick-looking magazine from the corporate world with which to impress future editors.

CHRISTINE FERGUSON
WORKING THE LOCAL MARKETS

You don't have to live in New York, Los Angeles, or any other megalopolis to make a career of freelance writing. Christine Ferguson has done quite well with the local markets in Fort Collins, Colorado, a mid-sized university town of under 100,000.

Not that it's easy. Publications in Fort Collins and thousands of smaller communities hardly pay *Redbook* or *Esquire* rates, so writers who prefer not to starve often have to shuck "magazine" mentalities and consider other markets like ad agencies, businesses, hospitals, government bureaus and anything else they can get.

Thanks to a varied background in small newspapers, computers, and medical research, Ferguson was able to branch out quickly when she turned to freelancing a few years ago. She also made a crucial discovery. "I always knew how to write and speak," she recalls. "But I had no personal subject area. Then I found that my area was helping *others* to write."

On an hourly basis, Ferguson works as a publicist for several private clients, including a woman who does management consulting. She writes sales training manuals for a Fort Collins branch of Hewlett-Packard and has written news releases for Colorado State University. Recently, she researched and wrote a grant application for the city, "Changing Our Minds About Poverty." In a career breakthrough, she wrote a textbook on cardiac rehabilitation with a local doctor and his staff. That led to further medical writing and a part-time job as contributing editor for *RT,* a respiratory therapy magazine.

She cultivates good clients, always trying to deliver immediate service so that they keep coming back. A weekly editorial column in the Fort Collins daily newspaper, *The Coloradoan,* gives her high visibility in town. "I'm always grateful that everyone isn't a good writer," she says, "because that's now *my* job."[12]

Now let's fast-forward a couple of years. I was progressing as a freelancer, following my curiosity (and sometimes the directive of an editor), and acquiring regular clients. Regular clients—whether they're national magazines or local hospital newsletters—are crucial to your well-being as a freelancer. Listen to what Cleveland, Ohio, freelance writer Frank Bentayou says about them:

After I've established a decent relationship with an editor—often through a steady stream of query letters—I find sometimes they cut me in on their needs more. They give me assignments, relieving me of the often-painful and time-consuming task of continuing to query them on stories. I have seldom turned down such assignments, even though some of them have not been my favorites. It's a matter of security; I usually could use the money, and I've been reluctant to risk alienating any editor who thinks enough of my work to call on me.[13]

One of my regular clients was *Chevrolet Friends,* which would later send me off hiking to Moab. One day the editor wondered if I'd like to do a monthly "back of the book" (inside the back cover) column: anything I wanted to write about, but 800 words maximum, and first person only. Fee: 50 cents per word. As a freelance writer who was paying all my own insurance and getting none of the other normal workplace benefits like retirement programs and paid vacations, who was I to say no?

Especially when I could once again crank out those boomerangs. Like this:

KING OF THE WIND

While I jealously watch, Chet Snouffer stands in a grassy field in Delaware, Ohio, and practices his 15,000-year-old art. He picks up a delicate-looking, delta-shaped stick, reaches back and . . .

And so I wove myself as a character into a truncated version of the third-person *Ohio* story that I'd originally written myself out of. Is it fair to mess around with the truth like this? Yes, because it isn't really messing around. For *Ohio*, I simply followed standard journalistic practice by removing the observer—me—from a scene I was really a part of. (And I don't care for the coy and dated convention of describing myself in a story as "a reporter.") For *Friends*, I simply described what I had actually done and felt.

This first-person version took just one evening. Soon the mail brought a check for Publication Number Three. Total: $1850.

Didn't *Friends* mind that some of the information had been published before? No. It goes out to a million people in fifty states and Canada; *Ohio* goes to 100,000 in one. Those are substantially different audiences. Besides, two years had passed.

Did I have to ask *Ohio* for permission to republish the original? Nope. The later version, transmogrified from third person to first and chopped to one-third the length, was *no longer* the original. More to the point, like most magazines and newspapers, *Ohio* routinely buys first rights only, which means that all control of the story, in any form, reverts to me upon publication. In other words, I'm free to do what I want with it.

By now I was getting tired of boomerangs. I was writing about other things, particularly ecology, and I'd moved to Colorado to teach at CSU. But soon enough I got a call from a *Quest Magazine* editor whom I'd worked with before. He was putting together a series of scrunchy little 300-word profiles called "Ordinary People, Extraordinary Dreams," about folks who'd dramatically changed their lives through willpower and hard work. If I knew anybody who fit the bill, he said, it might be worth $200.

Remember Ben Ruhe, the Smithsonian boomerang expert I mentioned in the *Marathon* story? Thanks to my "Booms" file, which was thick as a brick and still growing, I knew five or ten times more about him than I could squeeze into any one story. We had also been corresponding sporadically. Therefore, I happened to know that he had recently done something that sounded risky: quit the Smithsonian after a long career to freelance as a kind of Boomerang Everyman—lecturer, author, manufacturer, competitor.

AMBASSADOR OF BOOMERANGS

Like a boomerang, an old memory can swoop back home in the strangest way. For Smithsonian Institution staff writer Ben Ruhe, the memory *was* a boomerang, and it changed his life.

About 10 years ago . . .

With just a couple of hours of work, I had Publication Number Four. Total: $2050. That's $1600 more than I'd ever expected to get from this wacky topic. For the last three sales, I never even left the house!

I haven't written about boomerangs for quite a while, yet the file keeps growing. I come across odds and ends and stuff them in my file cabinet (my favorite piece of furniture), and readers of the articles have sent me jokes, anecdotes, reminiscences.

Recently someone sent me an announcement for this year's National Championships, to be held for the first time in Colorado. That'll be about two months from now, in a beautiful little mountain town. I keep telling myself that I'm bored with boomerangs, that I don't have time to go, but then again, if I just whip out a snappy query letter to *Outside*. . . .

*   *   *

Well, maybe not *Outside* after all. Just this morning they rejected, without comment, "Actors in the Sky."

So far, I've mailed out my lovingly written stunt artist story five times. Five new rejection slips sit in my drawer—five little deaths. Two contain encouraging handwritten words, three don't. Does this mean I've failed? It's much too soon to tell. A few months ago a friend of mine won a literary magazine's national fiction contest with a short story that had been rejected *thirty-seven* times. I won't let "Actors in the Sky" earn quite that many Frequent Flyer points before I do some rewriting, but I need to remind myself that a professional writer is also a professional stamp-licker and envelope-sealer. I'll send it out again this afternoon.

But first I'm going to change tactics. I'm going to forget about the large circulation magazines and the money that I'd hoped would help pay for all my slave labor. I'll shoot for what I think is the best of the literary magazines, *The Georgia Review*. Not that it's any easier of a target: in recent years it has published work by Robert Penn Warren, Joyce Carol Oates, and—amazingly enough—Robert Louis Stevenson (a long-lost manuscript). Not bad company.

And after all, part of the reason I decided to teach at a university was to let myself write about whatever I felt like, in whatever manner I thought appropriate. If my words didn't turn instantly to cash, that was okay, too (though it still hurts to say this). So off it will go to *The Georgia Review*, circulation five thousand, which does offer twenty-five dollars per printed page, but mainly pays off in prestige and personal satisfaction. The odds, as usual, are still stacked against me.

Meanwhile, I'm preparing to teach creative writing for the fast-approaching school year. I'm also proofreading the final manuscript of this book, fooling with the lead for a magazine feature on tropical rainforests in Asia (I flew to Thailand eight months ago but haven't been able to find time to write about it until now), and thinking about sending a poison pen letter to an editor who, without telling me, practically rewrote—and littered with clichés—a recent travel piece of mine. I'm angry, sad, happy, hopeful, excited, curious, content, frustrated, harried (for time, especially), and full of wonder at the possibilities of the world. In other words, I'm living the life of a freelance writer.

* * *

Well, there it is—an over-the-shoulder, impressionistic portrait of the way a freelance writer recognizes promising material, goes after it, "noodles," struggles, and transforms it into stories. Or at least it's a portrait of *this* freelance writer.

Again, not all of my still-evolving methods will work for you. At least, I hope they don't, because you've got to find your own way to be effective and please yourself as a writer. With luck, skill, talent, hard work, good guidance (I hope this book helped), and the rock-headed perseverance of a mule, you just might make it as a part- or full-time freelance writer.

Now get out there and give it a try.

* * *

P.S.

Ten weeks after finishing the final draft of this book and three full months after mailing off "Actors in the Sky"—BINGO! *The Georgia*

Review said yes! I'm thrilled, charged with renewed confidence for my new writing projects, and convinced, for at least the next few weeks, that writing is indeed a wonderful profession.

The letter of confirmation came last week. Yesterday I spoke on the phone with longtime *Georgia Review* editor Stanley W. Lindberg, who suggested small changes in the manuscript that he hoped would help the story "reach its full potential." Like these: "Why not use last names instead of first on repeated references to characters since using first names implies a familiarity that the writer usually doesn't have? . . . Movie titles should be italicized, not put in quotation marks. . . . On page one, the transition between your opening childhood memory and your visit to Moab years later might sound smoother if. . . . We wondered if the fourth sentence on page eleven might be stronger if it read like *this.*"

Here's what evolved from notes I made during that conversation—notes for a paragraph that was especially strengthened by the editors:

SUMMER, years later. The sun smashes me into the baked earth of Moab, Utah. I stand in a crowd, squinting up at a man in a red cape and a sweatshirt that says "Captain Action," teetering thirty feet above me on the ledge of a converted Mormon church. His name is John Hagner, and he is sixty years old. Nearby, two of his friends hold a ribbon over two piled-up air mattresses, the kind that pole vaulters fall into. When John crashes through the ribbon, three days of festivities will end, and the Hollywood Stuntmen's Hall of Fame will be open for business.

Obviously, Lindberg and his editors had read the manuscript very, very carefully. Every suggestion attempted to sharpen the focus of the story, not merely tinker with the kinds of word choices that reveal differences in voice between writer and editor. Almost immediately, I agreed with most of the suggestions. (Thus, my "final" version of the story that makes up chapter five has been slightly changed.) When I disagreed, I offered at least to consider the ideas when we got off the phone.

He will call back in a few days. (The hurried calls will help get the story into print before this book comes out; I assume *The Georgia Review* customarily works by mail.) Meanwhile, my copy of the manuscript sits before me on my desk. I bend over it and riffle through the pages, glancing now and then at the notes I made with Lindberg.

Let's see now, page eleven, fourth sentence. . . .

Good Books

Make room on your shelf for some of these books and magazines—collections of the best contemporary nonfiction, guides to research and writing, reference books.

BOOKS

Best American Essays. A new annual collection chosen from literary and commercial periodicals. 1987 guest editor Gay Talese's Introduction is a primer on "saturation reporting." 1988 editor Annie Dillard discusses the blurry lines between fiction and nonfiction. Features a list of journals that publish some of the finest literary nonfiction.

The Literary Journalists. Norman Sims, editor. An excellent anthology of the "art of reportage" including authors' comments and selections by Sara Davidson, Joan Didion, Tracy Kidder, John McPhee, Tom Wolfe, many others.

Our Times: Readings from Recent Periodicals. Robert Atwan, editor. Just what the title says, selections from *Esquire, Life, Ms, New York Times Magazine, Village Voice,* etc.

The Elements of Style. William Strunk, Jr., and E. B. White. That's the White who wrote *Charlotte's Web* and some of the most well-crafted personal essays in American letters. He learned the basics from Will Strunk, his college teacher. This 40-year-old pencil-slim collaboration is packed with sound advice about writing clear, controlled, straight-forward prose.

On Writing Well: An Informal Guide to Writing Nonfiction. William Zinsser. A joy to read. Full of witty and readable tips about common-sense writing and uncluttered style. Strunk and White's strongest competition.

Inventing the Truth: The Art and Craft of Memoir. William Zinsser, Editor. Six distinguished writers—Russell Baker, Annie Dillard, Alfred Kazin, Toni Morrison, Lewis Thomas, William Zinsser—discuss the pleasures and problems of trying to "reinvent the past."

Writing from Scratch: The Essay. John Clark Pratt. Whether you're a high school or college student, in the work force or retired, this lively, humorous, personal approach to essay writing shows you how writers *really* work. The how-to is built around a beautiful memoir of first love.

The Art of Fiction: Notes on Craft for Young Writers. John Gardner. The late novelist and teacher, author of *Grendel* and many other books, discusses how to plot, how to create character and tone. His writing exercises are especially good: "Describe a landscape as seen by a bird. Do not mention the bird." (What's a book about fiction doing in this nonfiction book? If you don't know by now, go back to chapter one and start over.)

From Fact to Fiction. Shelley Fisher Fishkin. A very readable study of five great imaginative writers who began their careers as journalists: Walt Whitman, Mark Twain, Theodore Dreiser, Ernest Hemingway, John Dos Passos. The last chapter is an excellent discussion of the ongoing debate that might be called "What is fact, what is fiction, and how important is the difference?"

Poison Penmanship: The Gentle Art of Muckraking. Jessica Mitford. Savagely witty and intelligent examples of research and organization strategies from a top investigative reporter.

The Complete Guide to Writing Non-Fiction. The American Society of Journalists and Authors. Invaluable advice and anecdotes from dozens of professionals. Arranged by topic: writing about the environment and energy, writing about food and nutrition, etc.

Writer's Market. The working nonfiction writer's bible. Contains thousands of listings of literary, commercial and popular marketplaces—

editors, addresses, payment rates, how-tos of manuscript preparation, sample query letters, etc. Essential.

How to Sell and Re-Sell Your Writing. Duane Newcomb. Forget the Nobel Prize for Literature; this is loaded with practical marketing ideas that can turn writing into a full-time job—a well-paying one. Typical chapters: "How to Fit Your Experience to a Magazine's Needs," "How to Turn Out Writing in Volume."

How to Sell 75% of Your Freelance Writing. Gordon Burgett. No Nobels here either, just lots and lots of good ideas for publishing your work.

The Literary Marketplace. Want to know if the *Miami Herald* accepts freelance feature articles, or if Viking Press publishes books about traveling in Europe? Look in this library reference work, which has an especially extensive list of city, regional, and small-town newspapers.

Working Press of the Nation. If you're wondering if IBM has a magazine that uses freelance feature stories about the hobbies of company employees, you'll find out in this three-volume reference that lists thousands of "in-house" publications not found in *Writer's Market* or anywhere else that I'm aware of.

MAGAZINES

Writer's Digest offers helpful inside looks at the lives of working writers, including lively first-person accounts from successful authors.

Columbia Journalism Review features readable, well-researched discussions about major issues in journalism, including ethics.

Editor & Publisher lists job opportunities for writers, reporters and editors.

Poets and Writers and *AWP Newsletter* do the same for poets, short story writers, novelists, and nonfiction writers. They also announce contests and grants and upcoming topical or "special issues" of magazines.

Endnotes

1. Annie Dillard, "Write Till You Drop," *New York Times Book Review*, 28 May 1989, p. 1.
2. E. B. White, "The Years of Wonder," *Essays of E. B. White* (New York: Harper & Row, 1977), p. 173.
3. Susan Goodman, telephone interview, August 1989.
4. "Behind the Byline," *Writer's Resource Guide*, 2nd ed. (Cincinnati: Writer's Digest Books, 1983), p. 321.
5. Tom Wolfe, "Author's End Note," *The Electric Kool-Aid Acid Test*, New York: Bantam, 1981, p. 371.
6. Gay Talese, *Best American Essays 1987* (New York: Ticknor & Fields, 1987), p. xiii.
7. Jon R. Luoma, telephone interview, August 1989.
8. Jessica Mitford, *Poison Penmanship* (New York: Farrar, Straus and Giroux, 1979), p. 13.
9. William L. Howarth, ed., *The John McPhee Reader*, 2nd ed. (New York: Random House, 1978), p. xvi.
10. Dillard, p. 23.
11. Tom Morrisey, letter to the author, June 1989.
12. Christine Ferguson, telephone interview, August 1989.
13. Frank Bentayou, letter to the author, June 1989.